RELIGION AND
RELIGIOSITY IN AMERICA

RELIGION AND RELIGIOSITY IN AMERICA

Studies in Honor of Joseph H. Fichter

EDITED BY
Jeffrey K. Hadden and Theodore E. Long

CROSSROAD · NEW YORK

1983
The Crossroad Publishing Company
575 Lexington Avenue, New York, N.Y. 10022

Printed in the United States of America

Library of Congress Cataloging in Publication Data
Main entry under title:

Religion and religiosity in America.

Contents: Joseph H. Fichter and the relevance of religion —
Religion and the construction of social problems /
Jeffrey K. Hadden — Cult formation / William Sims Bainbridge and Rodney Stark — [etc.]
1. United States — Religion — Addresses, essays, lectures.
2. Religion and sociology — United States — Addresses, essays, lectures.
3. Fichter, Joseph Henry, 1908-   — Addresses, essays, lectures.
I. Fichter, Joseph Henry, 1908-   . II. Hadden, Jeffrey K. III. Long, Theodore E.
BL2530.U6R4   1983   306'.6'0973   82-23605
ISBN 0-8245-0555-7

CONTENTS

RELIGION AND
RELIGIOSITY IN AMERICA

JOSEPH H. FICHTER, S.J.

Introduction:

JOSEPH H. FICHTER
AND THE RELEVANCE OF RELIGION

We address you, Lord God, as the bountiful Creator, the loving Provider, the vigilant Protector of all humanity. We thank You for all You have done for us, for the fellowship at this ICUS gathering across racial, national, and religious differences. We ask a blessing on this gathering, and on this food, and we pray that the poor, the underprivileged, and the unfortunate may receive also from Thy bounty. Amen.

THE beauty of this invocation is found not only in the eloquence and substance of the words and their appropriateness for the occasion on which they were offered, but also in the heart of the man from whose lips it came.

The prayer was offered by Father Joseph H. Fichter, a 73-year-old Jesuit sociologist from Loyola University of the South. The occasion was a banquet and gala performance for the grand opening of the Little Angels Performing Arts Center in a suburb of Seoul, Korea, in November 1981.

Two hours earlier, hundreds of happy Korean children in native costumes had braved the crisp autumn air to welcome with song the eight hundred guests from nearly a hundred nations as they arrived on the campus of The Little Angels Arts School. As the guests roamed freely about the campus to hear and see students perform, most felt the advance billing of the school as the "Julliard of Korea" had been no exaggeration.

It was a festive and moving moment when the burly Roman Catholic priest stepped to the podium on center stage of the gleaming new crimson bedecked concert hall. When his prayer moved beyond beseeching the Almighty's presence and blessing on the festive occasion to a petition on behalf of the poor and underprivileged of the world, it was a universal moment. Most of the men and women assembled were scientists. They were of every color and represented all the major faiths and ideologies of the world.

1

Yet for all the color and festivity, it was a troubling moment for many who were present. The pause for the invocation was a moment to remind many that they were not certain why they had been invited nor if they had done the right thing in accepting the invitation to attend the Tenth International Conference on the Unity of the Sciences, for which this was the closing ceremony.

Standing beside Father Fichter as he prayed was the founder of the school and the host of the conference and the banquet—the Reverend Sun Myung Moon. Offering the prayer of invocation at a gathering hosted by Reverend Moon was no big deal for Fichter. It had never crossed his mind that it would be best if he politely declined the invitation. To decline would have been most impolite.

Joseph Fichter is an unlikely candidate to become a champion of the teachings of Reverend Moon. He has studied Unification theology, and he is skeptical that God is fulfilling history in the manner taught by Reverend Moon. But Joseph Fichter is, and will remain, a champion of the rights of all to express freely their religious beliefs.

As a student of history, Father Fichter is aware of the similarities between the current cultural prejudice against Moonies and the anti-Catholic nativism that was rampant in the United States during the early 19th century.

Father Joseph Fichter has never consciously courted controversy. But neither has he walked away from a fight when there was a principle to uphold. When a New Orleans priest succeeded in having a sociological study suppressed in 1951, Fichter fought for a decade—all the way to the Vatican. This, in an era when censorship by the hierarchy of the Catholic Church was not uncommon. While the White Citizens Council and the Ku Klux Klan fought to block school desegregation in New Orleans, Fichter went quietly but openly about the business of teaching integrated classes of students from Loyola and Xavier universities. He was undaunted by the efforts of segregationists to check his influence on the Catholic Archdiocese—and ultimately greater New Orleans.

Fichter is not unaware that others often viewed him as a controversial figure and a trouble-maker. In his own memoirs, *One-Man Research,* he noted that "almost every time I tackled what I thought was a worthwhile ... problem, I seemed to get 'in trouble' " (Fichter, 1973:3). Indeed, his efforts to do what he believed right often led him to trouble. But it usually turned out that he was a one-man advance guard blazing a trail others would one day follow.

Andrew Greeley, years before he became America's most controversial Catholic priest, called Joseph Fichter a "pioneering giant." "It is easy to find fault with pioneering efforts," Greeley wrote, "but in the absence of pioneers the rest of us slow-moving mortals don't know where to go."

For nearly a half-century, Joseph Fichter has been pointing the way and showing us where to go as he has championed causes of social justice and human rights. He has been in the vanguard for social change regarding labor issues, integration, civil rights, women's roles, and church reform.

In the 1930s, he both defended organized labor and criticized corrupt union leadership; he advocated organization of white-collar workers; and he pleaded for more humane treatment of Mexican migrant laborers. In the 1940s, he quietly achieved the first desegregation of Catholic colleges in the deep south. In the early 1950s, he developed a strategy to desegregate the entire New Orleans' archdiocesan school system. When a White Citizens' Council blocked this, he launched a decade-long educational effort which finally succeeded. In the 1950s also, he wrote that reputed differences between the sexes are cultural in origin. Long a member of a Catholic women's rights group, he has advocated ordination of women priests since the late 1960s.

In the 1960s, Joe Fichter spent five years at Harvard as Stillman Professor. While in Cambridge, he maintained his deep involvement in civil rights struggles. His landmark study of police handling of arrestees in New Orleans was a first of its kind and helped call attention to police abuse against minorities and check that injustice. Also in the 1960s, he studied and recommended sweeping reforms regarding black colleges, lower echelon priests, the parochial education system, and sugarcane workers in Louisiana.

In the 1970s, Fichter's studies of charismatic Catholics contributed to an understanding of a phenomenon bewildering to millions of conventional Catholics. His study of alcoholic priests similarly addressed important questions of justice and human need. In his academic profession, he fought for the rights of woman sociologists and sought to engage the professional organizations of sociologists in the struggle to ratify the Equal Rights Amendment.

In sum, Joseph Fichter has never been indifferent to or afraid of controversial subjects. He has spent a lifetime quite literally jumping in where lesser men and women feared to tread.

Most sociologists struggle with a tension between objective scholarship and personal values. They, among all the social scientists, spend inordinate amounts of time arguing, perhaps more to convince themselves than others, that their discipline is value-free. Fichter has never wanted anything to do with the debate. He resolved this tension early and never swayed from his belief. He has never tried to convince anyone that his discipline nor his own sociological inquiries were value-free.

He has pursued a research career precisely because of his deep commitment to justice and human good. He believes that sociological research can illumine our understanding of human problems and, thus, help us know how to improve the human condition. And often research can call attention to social problems and human needs otherwise neglected.

Fichter would never concede that his passionate concern about human problems could possibly cloud his objectivity. "Because I am committed to a better society," he wrote in *One-Man Research*, "does not mean that I could eschew honest and objective reporting of research results" (Fichter, 1973:4).

Sociology, for Joseph Fichter, has been essentially an applied discipline. His career has reflected his position that sociological inquiry can help in identifying the nature and sources of injustice and suffering and that sociological insights can help in designing changes and formulating policy to better society and human life. He has been one of the most relentless data gatherers in American sociology, and his writings testify to his concerns. Thirty books, nearly two hundred articles, and dozens of unpublished reports comprise his research record and reflect his unswerving devotion to accumulating knowledge which addresses social needs.

For Joseph Fichter, there was nothing unique or unusual about his presence at a "Moonie conference" in Seoul, Korea, that autumn week during his 73rd year. He was grateful for the opportunity to attend conference sessions which expanded his knowledge of the Third World. And, as always when he attends scholarly meetings, he never skipped a session.

But Fichter had traveled half-way around the world, putting up with the fatigue of such a long journey, for a more important mission. He had become intrigued with the teachings of the Unification Church about marriage and the family. Not uncritical of Unification theology, nor oblivious to criticisms about their techniques of recruiting and tight regulation of members, Father Fichter wanted to learn about Unification Church family life through first-hand contact and interviews with church members. So, early in the mornings, late in the evenings, between sessions, and while others were enjoying leisurely dining, the workaholic priest could usually be spotted on a couch in some far corner of the hotel lobby with his tape recorder and a Moonie.

Father Joseph Fichter was in Korea doing what he had been doing for almost a half-century. He was there in hot pursuit of knowledge—knowledge he believed could be used for human betterment. Most likely, his religious superiors would have questioned the wisdom of his accepting the invitation to offer the invocation at the closing banquet. Awareness of this, had it occurred to him, would not likely have stopped him. Still, his prayer before this assembly was no more a belligerent defiance of authority than it was a legitimizing of the Reverend Sun Myung Moon. But in its calm and dignity, it may consciously have been a protest against the prejudices and hatreds of mankind.

The scholarly work of Joseph Fichter is too diverse and voluminous for easy classification, But Fichter's motivation for social science research is more easily identified. From his first major research project, *Southern Parish* (1951), through his more recent investigations of charismatics, alcoholic priests, and Unification Church members, Fichter has used research to identify problems in need of attention. A champion of many causes before they became identified as social problems, Fichter has also devoted attention to the internal problems of religious organizations. This latter concern, as we have come to understand it, is motivated by a desire to strengthen the church and its leadership to deal more effectively with social problems.

Fichter's interest in solving social problems is telescoped in his first book, *Roots of Change* (1939). Written almost a decade before he began his career as a sociologist, *Roots of Change* examines the lives of fourteen persons instrumental in shaping social change from the dawning of the Enlightenment through the end of the 19th Century. In that volume, Joe Fichter revealed his view of the individual in history:

For every thousand persons who are influenced by their own age, and shaped according to its mold, there is one person who harbors the dream of contributing his little share in reshaping the mold somewhat closer to his own ideal ... [a] person who feels a divine dissatisfaction with things as they are; who is determined that his own life and striving must not go down the vortex of popular and hysterical movements; who believes that he can bend ever so slightly by his efforts the onrush of a chaotic civilization (Fichter, 1929:vii).

One gets a strong sense that Fichter's decision to become a sociologist was motivated by a vision of how disciplined social scientific inquiry could contribute to the solution of social problems. Already the author of seven books, he entered graduate school at Harvard immediately after World War II and earned his doctorate in sociology in 1947 at age thirty-nine.

Both his tenacious commitment to permitting data to speak for themselves and his life-long career of spitting against the wind became well established in his first major research project. In January 1948, with ten undergraduate research assistants from Loyola University, Fichter set out on a short streetcar ride up river to Mater Dolorosa Parish. His guiding hypothesis was that the lives of these parishioners would be integrated by their Catholic beliefs and the life of the Church. What he found, instead, was that education and social class were barriers to the social integration of parish life. And secular ideologies were stronger forces in integrating urban Catholic parishioners than were common religious beliefs.

He was disappointed with his findings, but he was not about to "fudge" the data one iota. The pastor of the parish was furious and demanded that the study be suppressed. Fichter's provincial superior concurred and demanded consent of the parish pastor as a condition for granting approval to publish. During a decade-long struggle, that consent was never forthcoming. However, the University of Chicago Press had refused to halt publication of the first volume of *Southern Parish*, which was already in production when the controversy arose. But the other three volumes of *Southern Parish* have never been published.

Looking back, the whole episode appears too bizarre to have ever happened. But it did. In *One-Man Research*, Fichter wrote that he gave up the struggle not in a "spirit of humility and obedience," as requested by the Jesuit General, but rather in a "spirit of weariness and frustration" (Fichter, 1973:71). But the fact remains that while he may not have been humble, he remained obedient to his religious superiors.

Fichter has also always been a man of great resourcefulness. While he was fighting arbitrary censorship, he did visiting professorships at the University of Muenster in West Germany, the University of Notre Dame in Indiana, and the Catholic University of Santiago in Chile. In each institution he replicated a segment of the Mater Dolorosa Parish study. *Soziologie der Pfarrgruppen* (1958) and *Parochial School* (1958) reported the results of the replication studies conducted in Muenster and South Bend respectively.

Perhaps one reason Fichter's adversaries have always found him so frustrating is that he is always on the move. The huntsman knows that a moving target is hard to hit. And so does Joseph Fichter. But he never ran from a fight. He only shifted the battlefields to frustrate those who would have preferred a sitting target. And wherever he has moved, he has always found issues that demanded his attention, problems that needed solving.

The American Catholic Sociological Society had a special place in the life and career of Joseph Fichter. Created in 1938 by Catholic sociologists who wanted to set themselves apart from other American sociologists, the society was at once an object of admiration and for reform for Fichter when he joined a decade later. What Fichter admired about the group was its devotion to dealing with social issues and human needs. But he questioned the necessity and the wisdom of being Catholics apart from their roles as sociologists. He participated in other sociological organizations and encouraged non-Catholics to join ACSS.

Eventually, in the reform-minded years of the Second Vatican Council, Fichter's perspective prevailed. The American Catholic Sociological Society jettisoned its Catholic identity and chose, instead, the sociological study of religion as its *raison d'etre*. Catholic members uninterested in the study of religion per se drifted from the organization. At the same time, the newly constituted organization, known as the Association for the Sociology of Religion, found itself searching for an identity which differentiated it from the interdisciplinary Society for the Scientific Study of Religion and the then highly applied Religious Research Association.

In 1978, with the assistance of several graduate students at the University of Virginia, we undertook a social history of the organization which led us to the early volumes of the *American Catholic Sociological Review* and their detailed organizational minutes and annual meeting program notes. We concluded that interest in solving social problems traversed the history of the organization. At the onset, theological conviction pretty much defined various Catholic postures toward social problems. But the predominance of theological opinion over scientifically derived knowledge began to be challenged after World War II, a period corresponding with the education of Catholic sociologists like Joseph Fichter and Joseph Fitzpatrick in some of the better graduate departments of secular institutions. What we failed to find was any break in the underlying assumptions that knowledge is useful in identifying and understanding problems of social structure and human suffering and, moreover, this knowledge should be put to work to reduce social ills.

Our reason for pursuing this historical investigation was that we were respectively president-elect and program chair-designate for the Association for the Sociology of Religion, 1979. We wanted a meeting theme which would be appropriate for honoring Joseph Fichter on his 70th birthday. We were convinced of the appropriateness of social problems as an integrating theme for the career research of Fichter. We had no idea that this theme would also be so consistently carried on in the life and history of the organization.

The only problem which remained was to see whether members would respond to the program theme, ''Religion and the Construction of Social Problems.'' They did, in numbers and ways that far exceeded our expectations. We had a record number of papers presented and a record attendance for the period since the organization had changed its name and emphasis in the mid-1960s. And, quite probably, we had a record proportion of papers presented which dealt with some dimension of the program theme.

Our initiative in putting together a program which would honor Joseph Fichter served only to magnify our own intellectual debt to him. Our pursuit of the social problems theme as an integrative concept for *his* work has now become a dominant perspective for the theoretical integration of *our* own. Our individual contributions, and the way we have endeavored to tie together the contributions of our colleagues, provide but a skeleton upon which we hope to construct new frameworks for thinking about social problems.

There exists an inexorable relationship between religion and that which contemporary civilization defines as problematic. How these laws govern our world are yet unknown. But thanks to Fichter, we have affixed our sociological microscopes on the right subject matter.

Most of the papers for this *Festschrift* honoring Joseph H. Fichter emerged from the 1979 annual meeting of the Association for the Sociology of Religion. We are pleased that a meeting which was planned to honor a man of such stature can live on in this way. We regret only that space limitations and an effort to provide substantive continuity prohibit inclusion of more of the fine papers which were presented at that meeting.

To some, Joseph Fichter will be remembered as a sociological gadfly, jumping always from one issue to another without lingering to harvest the bounty he discovered. A restless pioneer, the continuity in his work seemed to be the fact that he identified issues and problems that others who followed would scrutinize more thoroughly. When Gauguin admonished van Gogh for painting too fast, the Dutchman retorted, "You look too fast!" We are persuaded that those who fail to find continuity and integration in Fichter's work have looked too fast.

Continuity is found in Fichter's work in at least three important ways. We have already identified his compassionate concern for utilizing sociological methods to identify social problems and human needs. A second point of continuity is that his concern with social problems has always been informed by broader theoretical concern for the fundamental problems of sociological knowledge.

How is social order possible? How do individual and society relate to form a social order? Examples of this concern may be found in Fichter's first major sociological investigation, the *Southern Parish,* which focuses on solidarity and anomie in an urban parish. His present research on the Unification Church addresses the fundamental sociological question of how the family contributes to the organization of sustaining social life. So a man passionately driven by the desire to *change* society in ways that will produce human betterment has an intellectual gyroscope which never ceases to ask how *order* is sustained.

Another point of continuity in Fichter's work is that he has never lost track of the relevance of religion to human societies. Our social scientific theories of secularization, couched in evolutionary presuppositions, have encouraged us to forget that religion has always been relevant. Fichter did not forget. Religion can be a stubborn barrier to change. But it can also provide the dynamo that makes change possible.

We struggled to make sense of all the sociological investigation which could be broadly classified under the rubric of religion and social problems: religion as the constructor of social problems; religion as the legitimizer of the existence of certain social problems; religion as the solution to social problems; and religion as a social problem. In all of this, it was only the sense that religion was *relevant* which gave continuity to the flurry of investigations which linked social problems and religion.

What we struggled so long to grasp was the rather simple proposition that how religion is relevant may be changing. Had our quest remained truer to the clues provided in the work of Joseph Fichter, our task of discovery would have been much less painful.

The nexus of religion's relationship to social problems lies in the antagonism between individual and society around which modern American life revolves. Religion is linked to this process both by its own moral interests and by others' interests in appropriating the moral resources of religion on behalf of individual or society. In that regard, religion has *always* been relevant to social problems. What is new is the specific type of relevance it enjoys, which reflects its shifting allegiance from society to individuals.

Traditionally, religion has spoken for the collectivity, affirming the interests of society over those of egoistic individuals. As analyzed here, however, the new movements in religious life favor the individual, asserting society's responsibility to support and sustain the person against the perils of modern life.

That new approach to social influence can be seen most clearly in the new religions, the new evangelical politics, and the involvement of religion with new therapies for troubled souls. The individual papers on these topics focus on specific aspects of these developments. Before turning to them, however, we elaborate our general interpretation of the new relevance as a context for grasping their significance.

First, we summarize the idea of individual-society relations people use in the modern world. Second, we show *how* people use those ideas to formulate problems and to define preferred solutions. Finally, we show how current religious phenomena fit in those schemes and what they signify for religion in modern society.

As it is usually understood, the problem of individual and society rests on two beliefs. First, we trust that the "individual" and "society" are real entities, each with distinct characteristics, whose cooperation is necessary for human life. Second, we believe that the two cannot be relied upon to cooperate because one or the other will be either unwilling or unable to do so. In either case, normal social life depends on one dominating the other, and every formulation of the issue expresses some sympathy for and confidence in one over against the other.

The conception of individual and society came to prominence in the transformation of western life variously known as industrialization, urbanization, modernization, rationalization, and sometimes secularization. However named and defined, those revolutionary processes were enormously disruptive of established life. People knew neither what was happening nor what was coming, only that they had lost the traditional life they believed to have been part of God's creation. With respect to the organization of their lives, the chaos posed two major difficulties, one *cognitive* and the other *moral*.

Cognitively, people no longer understood the social world. They did not know who was powerful, what was important, or even what to call some things. And because they couldn't explain how anything worked or why, they did not even know how to take control of events to normalize their lives. Morally anomic, people no longer knew how to tell right from wrong or how to allocate credit and blame. The rules were uncertain, and worse, there was no moral authority to guide them through the turmoil. Even the gods who had previously guaranteed knowledge and morality were suddenly not so trustworthy, if people believed they were present at all.

Eventually, people settled on individual and society as the pivotal categories around which they reorganized their cognitive and moral worlds. Cognitively, those ideas expressed the ordinary citizens' experience of being alone and unprotected against invisible, distant forces controlling their lives. Those powerful figures whose positions had been undercut by modernization also found the ideas useful to express their sense that they (society) were losing control over troublemakers (individuals). Notice that each *perception* of the individual-society connection centers on some *wrong* and the force which caused it. Indeed, the explanatory value of these ideas seems to have derived from their moral attribution of blame for suffering inflicted. Later, people would attribute to these forces moral credit for preventing the other's mischief, but the original emphasis on harm and blame had already defined the idea.

If all that seems a bit abstract, it is not surprising, because people came to use the ideas of individual and society virtually as theological categories. Those who had abandoned the gods used these invisible forces as substitutes for them. Those who still believed assimilated these new forces to their own pantheon. Cognitively, these ideas went beyond mere description to ontology; morally they moved beyond right and wrong to define generative sources of good and evil. In many ways, therefore, they came to function as religious ideas; when they did not, they engaged real religious sentiments at the deepest level as the terms through which religion expressed its concerns about the culture around it.

Those basic contours of the individual-society conception largely define its possible uses in formulating and responding to social problems in modern society. Defining something as a problem constitutes an accusation that cooperation between individual and society has broken down to the detriment or harm of one or the other. Naturally, people do not define problems in these abstract terms; they blame specific people or institutions for tangible harm they or their allies suffer. But who they blame and what they accuse them of depends on their conception of individual and society, along with the events in question.

TABLE 1

SOCIAL PROBLEMS OF INDIVIDUAL-SOCIETY AND THEIR PREFERRED SOLUTIONS

Sympathy for Society	
Problems	*Solution*
1. Individual Underconformity	Education of Individual
2. Individual Deviance	Regulation of Individual

Sympathy for Individual	
Problems	*Solution*
1. Insufficiency of Society	Reorganization of Society
2. Overregulation by Society	Objectivization of Society

Those who identify with society are concerned with *individual conformity* to norms and to orders. They usually explain troubling conditions by reference to some flaw in the individual(s) who caused them to happen. There are two ways for individuals to go wrong: by overstepping the bounds of authority or norms to commit an *unapproved (deviant) act,* or by failing to fulfill one's obligations to others (identified with society), which we call *underconformity.*

In contrast, when people identify with the individual, they are concerned with the *social support* they receive, and trouble calls forth a critique of social institutions as the culprit(s). Institutions may also fail in two ways: by not giving individuals sufficient backing for their actions, which we call *societal insufficiency,* or by *overregulating* the individual, that is, controlling more than necessary. Table 1 summarizes these four main types of individual-society problems.

That same table also shows the preferred solutions to these problems. In the case of underconformity, the task is to *educate* the individual to instill the capacity or motivation to live up to expectations. Unapproved (deviant) acts, however, are met with penalty and punishment, the main forms of *regulation.* When society fails the individual through some insufficiency, it requires more *organization,* which can take the form of legislating new rules or redistributing resources. Finally, because overregulation implies a failure to acknowledge the legitimacy of the individual's action, it requires that the reasons for conduct be strengthened, or *objectified* in the public mind.

To show how these abstractions come to life, consider how the problem of unemployment would be construed from these various standpoints. Those who

identify with society would surely blame the unemployed workers themselves for their plight, either for failing to prepare well enough and to
search hard enough for work (underconformity) or perhaps for drinking so
much as to prompt firing, striking illegally, and the like (unapproved acts).
To alleviate the condition, the former group would need job training or
motivation classes, while the latter would require some punishment to keep
it from happening any more. However, those who favor the individual
would see the problem differently, as a failure of society to support the
worker. Too few jobs would count as an insufficiency requiring the reorganization of work, while authoritarian supervision or rules preventing people
from working over a certain age would be seen as overregulation which
prompts the unemployed to demonstrate the objective validity of their
viewpoints.

That nonreligious example makes clear the importance of sympathies for
this matter of individual and society relations. In the case of religion, its new
relevance arises directly from its *shift of sentiment away from society toward
the individual*. That means more than simply changing sides, for it alters
fundamentally the manner in which religion enters public life in modern
society. Instead of holding individuals to account for their conformity to
(sacred) societal authority, religion now asserts the individual right to be
sustained, supported, and even subsidized by society. This *moral entitlement
approach* to social problem formation takes two forms. The first faults society
for not supplying sufficient backing for religious and moral practice. The
second is critical of society for denying individual liberty and for overenforcing
conformity to societal norms, as if they were religious. In the latter, religion
now resists what once was considered its own primary social role; in the
former, it reverses traditional roles so that society justifies religion, not vice
versa.

The significance of this shift emerges more clearly when we contrast it with
religious social protest in the 1960s and the much heralded "privatization" of
religion. Both appear in some way to serve individual against society, but
neither actually does so. Both were allied with society, but in different ways.
The social protest was a prophetic one in which religion held the individuals in
society accountable to ideal norms, presumably already in place in our political
charters (e.g., civil rights). Moreover, those protests often took the side of the
state explicitly against individual violators of civil rights. These crusades, in
short, supported collective norms in a drive against underconformity. Privatization represents an even clearer case of alliance with society because it
presents no critique of existing order. It merely enjoys obscurity of the private
world and leaves public life to operate on its own without critical examination.
From the vantage point of the new relevance, privatization just gets the

individual out of society's way, and that neglect would qualify as insufficient societal support.

We see this new relevance of religion most clearly in the three phenomena singled out for attention in this volume: new religions, new religious politics, and new therapeutics. That this unlikely lot should find itself together in support of the individual is not to say that they are allies, for they are often at odds over particular issues. But they do share a common cultural method for establishing the relevance of the sacred to the world and for taking action to realize that relevance.

1. The burst of *new religious movements* whose eccentricities and excesses captured our attention in the 1970s has often been attributed to the failure of established institutions to supply adequate meaning for the individual. That account constitutes a primitive claim to moral and spiritual entitlement which sustains a whole complex of related attitudes and practices. As Bird notes, for example, cult life also *discourages* a sense of moral accountability to society, and new religions defend themselves against accusations of impropriety not by showing to the contrary but by asserting their religious liberty.

2. The new *evangelical politics* also constitutes an entitlement approach, except it favors traditional morality where new religions often criticize it. On the one hand, evangelicals criticize society for not enforcing the traditional moral principles they have adopted on issues of sex, famiy life, etc. On the other hand, they chafe and rail at societal regulation, in schools for example, which to their minds denies them liberty to do things their traditional way. Those who wonder how they can be for liberty and also against it should note that it may be less a matter of liberty than of loyalty, in this case loyalty to the individual rather than to society and its claims.

3. In contrast both to new religions and to evangelical politics, the *new therapy* considered here has a secular flavor, by virtue of which it appears to align itself with society, not the individual. Conventionality, though, is not the issue here; sympathies are. And the sympathies of the new healing arts lie clearly with the individual. The maladies diagnosed in the new religious therapy are attributed directly to the failure of society both to support and to protect the individual. The aim of therapy is to secure happiness and satisfaction for the patient/client in spite of society. It represents, in fact, a certain resignation about society's failures, which suggests that religion's sympathies for society may wane even more in the future than they have already.

We have no crystal ball, however, and the future of these intriguing movements is still very cloudy. We can anticipate only that the near future will see an intensification of religious conflict, among religious groups themselves and also between religion and other segments of society. Conflict of the former type used to be an intramural sport of sorts, but now religious groups confront each other across a gulf of opposing loyalties to individual and society. The latter conflicts are also perennial, but they too have changed. Once religion abandons its loyalty to society, it is possible for others to see it as an instance of deviance or underconformity. For many, then, religion itself will be a social problem. Whatever happens, we believe the study of religion's relevance to the problems of human life will continue to be a most fruitful field for scholars to cultivate, just as it has been and continues to be for Father Joe Fichter.

References

Fichter, Joseph H., 1939. Roots of Change. New York: Appleton-Century.

Fichter, Joseph H., 1951. Southern Parish: Dynamics of a City Church. Chicago: University of Chicago Press.

Fichter, Joseph H., 1958. Soziologie der Pfarrgruppen. Muenster: Aschendorf.

Fichter, Joseph H., 1958. Parochial School: A Sociological Study. Notre Dame, Indiana: University of Notre Dame Press.

Fichter, Joseph H., 1973. One-Man Research: Reminiscences of a Catholic Sociologist. New York: Wiley and Sons.

I

The New Relevance of Religion

1

RELIGION AND THE CONSTRUCTION OF SOCIAL PROBLEMS

Jeffrey K. Hadden

INTRODUCTION

Reflecting upon two thousand manuscripts processed during six years as editor of *Social Problems* (1969-75), David Gold recently examined the relationship between social research and social problems (Gold, 1979). He concluded that the relationship is fuzzy and that this is so because the bulk of the research is not very good. My investigation into religion and social problems reveals not so much a plethora of bad research as a failure to link the two concepts together at all. While a considerable body of literature is germane to the topic, I located nothing approaching a systematic statement about the relationship between religion and social problems.

In choosing "Religion and the Construction of Social Problems" as the program theme for our annual meetings, I also accepted the challenge of attempting a conceptual link between the two concepts. Had I known then what I have learned since selecting the theme, I'm certain I would have had second thoughts. The relationship between religion and social problems is substantially more complex and subtle than I had imagined. What I offer is but a prolegomenon to a systematic theoretical statement on the relationship between religion and social problems. In getting even this far, I am now more persuaded than when I began of the importance of developing a systematic statement, and I hope this effort will persuade others.

This paper seeks to accomplish three tasks. The first is to examine the role of religion in defining and dealing with social problems in an historical context. This requires an understanding of the changing relationship between religion and political regime. In pursuit of this objective, I shall show that prior thinking about the relationship has been thwarted by concepts loaded with value presuppositions.

17

The second task is to identify the importance of defining key concepts. The absence of consensus about definitions has contributed to the failure to develop theory. Drawing upon important recent work in both areas, I shall suggest definitions to key concepts.

The third task is to identify *elements* of a conceptual framework for developing theory. This effort is a first approximation or a scaffolding which may be useful for the work that lies ahead. Scaffolding, understand, is but a temporary structure from which something more durable might be constructed. If I have erected it in the correct location, perhaps others will join in the construction work.

HISTORICAL CONTEXT:
THE CHANGING ROLE OF RELIGION IN SOCIAL PROBLEMS

For two reasons, it is important to examine in historical context the role of religion in defining and dealing with social problems. First, the relationship between religion and political regime has changed dramatically over the past four hundred years. This change, in turn, has had profound effects on the role of religion in the definition and resolution of social problems. Contrary to the assumption that religion has played a diminishing role in modern society, I want to argue that its role in defining and resolving social problems has intensified. Second, our traditional concepts to deal with religion and change do not serve well in considering social problems. Indeed, the concepts themselves have a latent analytical bias which I believe has contributed to our failure to recognize the role of religion in defining and resolving social problems in the modern era.

In traditional society, we expect to find religious institutions embracing the world view offered by the political regime. In modern societies, however, the church may be aligned with the interests of the state *or* it may stand in radical opposition. This fact has been obscured by our theoretical constructs. Consider first our preoccupation with the *church-sect* typology. In one of the clearer delineations of these concepts, Johnson defines church as "a religious group that accepts the social environment in which it exists," and "a sect is a religious group that rejects the social environment in which it exists" (Johnson, 1963:542).

This conceptualization allows for tension between the state and sects, but it assumes a rather tension-free relationship between church and state. This conceptual bias leads to the view that disruptions of harmony between church and state are aberrations.

I propose we would be better served by quite a contrary assumption, namely that latent tension between the state and religious institutions is inherent in their structural relationships. Manifest tension will erupt periodically in disputes over social problems because the master or dominant roles of church and state are structurally incompatible.

To understand when, where and why religious institutions will become involved in social problems and place themselves in confrontation with the state, we need to grasp the changing power relationships between the two over the past several hundred years. Berger's treatise, *The Sacred Canopy* (1967), represents an important synthesis of efforts to analyze the changing relationship between church and state as society has been transformed from a simple agrarian world to a complex industrial-technological order.

The central thrusts of Berger's argument are rather well known to sociologists of religion, so I shall merely sketch those features essential to my argument. Central to Berger's theory is the distinctive place of religion in legitimizing man's precarious world-building enterprise. Recall also that the central fact of modern history has been the erosion of the power of religion to legitimate the social order. This is so, Berger argues, because of *secularization*, "the process by which sectors of society and culture are removed from the domination of religious institutions" (Berger, 1967:107), and *pluralism,* a cognitive corollary to secularization.

Modern man no longer possesses a monolithic world view articulated by the tenets of religious faith. Rather, he "is confronted with a wide variety of religious and other reality-defining agencies that compete for his allegiance, or at least attention, and none of which is in a position to coerce him into allegiance" (Berger, 1967:126). The process of secularization, thus, has altered fundamentally the relationship between religion and political regime. *To speak of secularization is to speak of the separation of church and state.*

Conventional wisdom sees secularization as gradually eroding the resources of religious institutions as the plausibility structures of their doctrines are undermined in a pluralistic society. Religion loses ground not only to the state but also to other reality-defining sectors of modern society. This prospect worried the great French theoretician Durkheim (1965) so much that he feared society would crumble for want of an integrative force. Berger is not quite so pessimistic, but clearly he sees religion on the defensive, reacting to rather than shaping the great forces of history.

The impact of secularization in modern societies is an historical fact of inestimable significance. At the same time, conceiving of secularization as an inevitable unilinear erosion of religious influence in culture, leading to the eventual demise of religious organizations, is an ill-conceived idea that is overdue for a quiet burial.

Alternatively *secularization should be viewed as merely a process which has broken the historical link between church and state.* While it appears to be an inevitable outcome of the industrial-technological revolution, we ought not assume the process to be identical, or even very similar, in all societies. To assume a process of secularization modeled after Western Europe and the United States is to ignore the great variability within those geo-political units. And how are we to integrate Israel or Japan into a single unilinear model of secularization? The obvious answer is that they don't fit very well.

To summarize, the process whereby church and state became separate sectors of society simultaneously and inevitably created a tension between the two. From a sociology of knowledge perspective, two conceptual ideas in the social scientific study of religion have served to camouflage this critical historical change. The *church-sect typology* has tended to reinforce the traditional view of religion as a handmaiden of the state and its dominant value system. The theoretical ideas associated with the concept *secularization* have projected the demise in the power and authority of religious institutions and belief systems to give direction and meaning to modern social systems. A direct implication of these interlocking theoretical biases is that religion is relatively impotent in the face of the major social problems of the modern world.

To correct this conceptual bias, a framework is needed for examining the role of religion in the definition and resolution of social problems without preconceptions about the nature of its influence. The third section of this paper attempts to identify elements of such a conceptual framework. This follows a discussion of the problem of defining key concepts, our next task.

THE PROBLEM OF DEFINING KEY CONCEPTS

The links among theory, propositions, concepts, and definitions are critical to the development of science. Fuzzy definitions of vague concepts lead to imprecise propositional statements and theory of limited utility. Without good theory, we accumulate facts with little understanding of how they go together or how to shake out undesirable material. All disciplines suffer to some degree from inadequate definitions and concepts, but some have greater deficiencies than others. And, within disciplines, some subspecialties have greater conceptual difficulties than do others.

Both the sociology of religion and the study of social problems are plagued with critical conceptual problems. Commenting on the state of the sociology of religion, Stark and Bainbridge (1979:117) recently wrote " ... if the purpose of concepts is to serve as primary terms for theories, little progress has been made." Spector and Kitsuse (1977:1) are even harsher in their recent critique of theory in social problems: "There is no adequate definition of social problems within sociology, and there is not now and never has been a sociology of social problems.'' Very much to the benefit of their respective inquiries, Stark and Bainbridge, working in the sociology of religion, and Spector and Kitsuse, working in the study of social problems, have pointed us in the direction to greater conceptual clarity of key ideas.

Let us begin with religion. Stark and Bainbridge view the concept *compensators* as pivotal for the reconstruction of a systematic set of concepts in the sociology of religion. "Compensators,'' they write, "are postulations of reward according to explanations that are not readily susceptible to unambiguous evaluation'' (Stark and Bainbridge, 1979:120). They hasten to add that nothing pejorative is implied by the term. "Compensators merely refer to postulations of reward based on hope and faith rather than in knowledge.'' Working from this perspective, then, religion may be understood as '' ... *a system of general compensators based on supernatural assumptions''* (Stark and Bainbridge, 1979:121). Religious institutions are engaged in the business of production and exchange of general compensators.

While a linguistically radical departure from prior definitions, this is a much less radical conceptual transformation than appears at first glance. It retains the critical sociological content of other definitions of religion, yet it eschews nonessential theological baggage and differentiates religion from other sources of insight about "ultimate meaning.'' And it takes for granted the centrality of theodicy for religion.

Spector and Kitsuse define social problems as *"the activities of individuals or groups making assertions of grievances and claims with respect to some putative conditions,"* (Spector and Kitsuse, 1977:75). This definition shifts the subject matter of social problems from conditions in society to the *response* of individuals or groups to those conditions. Poverty, crime, prejudice, and a whole host of other things which may be judged objectively as deleterious to society are not, in themselves, social problems. They become social problems only when significant forces in society treat them as such.

This definition breaks with traditional conceptions of social problems that focus on what is assumed to be problematic. By focusing on the *activities* of individuals and groups, the Spector and Kitsuse approach de-emphasizes the alleged putative condition to the point where it almost becomes insignificant. The importance of the putative condition needs to be restored without giving it primacy. Moreover, an adequate definition of a social problem needs to incorporate the notion of the *effectiveness* of those asserting grievances and claims. Otherwise, almost everything in society is some individual's or group's social problem. From this perspective we can study what types of persons or groups perceive what kinds of social phenomena as problematic. But I think this falls short of a universalistic construct which is capable of forming the foundation for the development of systematic theory.

In an effort to correct these shortcomings in the Spector and Kitsuse definition, I propose the following modification:

A social problem is a social phenomenon identified as intolerable by powerful individuals or institutions and subsequently made the object of a mobilization of resources to effect change.

The significance or seriousness of the social problem can be measured by the mass of collective energy aimed at initiating or sustaining change-directed activity. An operational definition of power is simply the ability to present the issue to the public over a sustained period of time.

This definition of social problems is closely akin to the concept social movements, particularly as the latter has developed around the notion of resource mobilization. This coincidence is not accidental. When resources are being mobilized to draw attention to a problem and to pressure the state to recognize the legitimacy of claims, social problems and social movements can be essentially identical. In other phases in the life of a social problem, social movements are not a feature of the problem.

I propose that social movements be viewed as a particular type of problem-solving activity. Mass media are capable of identifying something as a social problem without any support from social movements. Similarly, persons and organizations of great power (economic and political) are capable of defining social problems. But most social problems result from organized efforts by those who define some issue(s) as intolerable. They may do so because they are personally affected, or they may press grievances on behalf of others.

In the life history of social problems that persist over a period of time, social movements are important in defining and pressing appropriate parties to action. And, social movements may be involved in evaluating the effectiveness of problem-solving activity. Often, however, the strength of social movements has dissipated before structures designed to solve problems have been set in motion. Those who initially allege intolerable conditions may have to reorganize a social movement if the activities designed to effect change are to be evaluated. In other cases, social movements become an institutionalized permanent feature of society. While a number of civil rights groups have survived the social movements stages relating to race relations, organized labor is a better example of permanent institutionalization of a social movement.

ELEMENTS OF A CONCEPTUAL FRAMEWORK

Understanding when, why, and how religious institutions will become engaged in social problems involves a complex set of variables and contingencies. Some variables will be easy to measure, others present difficulties, and some perhaps only can be approximated. The process whereby religious institutions become involved in social problems will not be understood until (1) the salient factors affecting the probability of involvement are identified and (2) their relative impacts are measured and assessed.

In this section I shall attempt to identify factors which seem conceptually relevant to the issue of religious involvement in social problems. Many of the factors identified are, of course, relevant to the involvement of any institution. I shall focus attention on those variables unique to religious institutions.

Three fundamental questions need to be addressed in analyzing whether, why, and how a religious institution will become involved in a social problem. First, what *interests* of the religious institution are at stake in the issue which has been or is about to be labeled as problematic? Second, what *resources* does the religious institution have that might be invested? Third, what are the *organizational features* of the religious institution which will facilitate or impede engagement?

Interests. The interests of religious institutions may be considered to be four in kind: (1) survival, (2) economics, (3) status, and (4) ideology. A threat, or perceived threat, to any of these will likely lead to some response. The greater the perceived or actual threat, the greater the effort to mobilize resources to respond. The *ideological* dimension is singled out for comment here since this dimension most clearly differentiates religious institutions from other organizations in society.

The ideological dimension of religious institutions includes both a *reservoir of cultural values and ideas* and a *system of transcendental moral values, customs, and laws*. Both levels represent a basis for structural strain between church and state. The former results from a "natural" division of labor between church and state and the latter from the necessity of protecting transcendental interests from encroachment by either secularization or a hostile state.

Man's hopes and ideals outstrip his ability to accomplish; always there are gaps between visions of what might or ought to be and what is. Many social institutions are carriers of visions and dreams not realized, but religious institutions play a special role, for it is here that dreams are transformed into the will of deities.

Societies normally live quite comfortably with the incongruities between their creeds and deeds. When the gap is identified as no longer tolerable, however, we have the root of an emerging social problem. We also have a structural condition that is likely to produce strain between religion and state. This is so for a number of reasons.

Most importantly, in modern societies the resolution of most social problems is assumed to rest with government. Or the government itself may be labeled as the social problem for its failure to deal satisfactorily with issues that have gained collective recognition as intolerable. Whatever other roles, obligations, and goals the state may assume through time, it has primary responsibility for preserving order. This tends to make governments conservative and resistant to change. Social problems represent contradictory claims about social order. Groups that want to change something are usually met by opposition from those who would keep things as they are. The state, in the role of arbitrator, is likely to be cautious and resistant to change even when the interests of the state may not be at stake.

Religious institutions in a secular society, on the other hand, are under no inherent obligation to uphold the status quo. Their interests may rest in maintaining the status quo, or they may not. But as carriers of ideologies and ideals, religious institutions may have an interest in change. They may even be instrumental in defining some social phenomena as problematic and in taking the initiative in mobilizing resources to change that which has been defined as intolerable. Whether or not religious institutions take the initiative in defining social problems, they are likely to face pressure to support change in the name of values or ideals hoped for.

In short, the historical relationship between church and state was one of mutual reinforcement. In the modern secular world, built-in structural forces tend to generate pressure to place church and state in tension over social problems. We can even go one step further and state that it was secularization that gave religious institutions a role in identifying and pressing social problems grievances.

In addition to religious institutions' having an interest in the cultural values and ideals of society, they also have an interest in preserving and protecting their own transcendental moral values, customs, and laws. When there is considerable coincidence between their transcendental precepts and the values, laws, and life styles of the larger society, protection is not likely to be a major issue. The greater the variance between the two, the greater the resources that must be invested in protecting transcendental interests.

Protective activities may be either *defensive* or *offensive*. The former attempt to hold off the onslaught of secular culture and other reality-defining institutions, while the latter endeavor to remake society in ways more compatible to the transcendental values of the group's religion.

Resources. Next we turn to the question of the kinds of resources religious institutions may be able to bring to bear in dealing with a social problem. The potential resources of religious institutions include (1) economic assets, (2) leadership, (3) manpower, and (4) legitimacy conferring powers. It is the last which differentiates the resources of religious institutions from those of other organizations which might get involved in social problems.

In assessing resources, it should be recognized that an inventory is not an indicator of the capacity of an institution to mobilize and commit resources. The ability to commit resources is a function of organizational structure, leadership skills, degrees of consensus and dissensus among members, etc.

Generally, institutional engagement in a social problem involves a series of progressive escalations from little or no involvement to extensive involvement. In their provocative article on resource mobilization and social movements, McCarthy and Zald (1977:1223) differentiate among *bystander publics, adherents,* and *constituents.* A resolution of support for a cause, however generally or vaguely stated, moves an organization from the status of a bystander to that of an adherent; that is, the group has gone on record affirming that some social phenomenon is undesirable, that some proposal to deal with a problem has merit, etc. Those within the institution who support the social problem cause will then endeavor to move the organization from the role of an adherent to that of a constituent. Once this is achieved, the application of resources is officially begun.

With respect to leadership, manpower, and economic support, religious organizations are no different from other organizations which might become involved in social problems. *The unique role of religious institutions is their potential to confer legitimacy both on the definition of some phenomenon as problematic and on specific activities pursued in the struggle to gain recognition for the definition.*

One important consequence of secularization, we have seen, is the erosion of the authority of religious institutions to confer legitimacy. Other reality defining institutions compete with religion to answer the questions *why* and *what ought to be.* But neither the erosion of the plausibility structures on which religion is based nor the competition from other sectors of society strips religious institutions of their portfolios of creditable stock.

The ability to proclaim successfully that "God is on our side" is a significant resource in the struggle to define and press social problem claims. However, the sheer fact that a religious institution or leader supports a social problem cause does not assure the cause's being legitimated in the minds of a significant public. This will depend on (1) the generalized level of authority of religious leaders in the society in question (and/or the particular authority of the leader or institution proclaiming support), (2) whether the message that is being communicated is consistent with the receivers' general value orientations, (3) the degree to which the receivers of the message perceive the message as consistent with their own interest, and (4) the degree to which theological ideology is perceived as unambiguously relevant and clear on the issues(s). The receivers need not be church members or even believers to be convinced or reinforced by the conferral of legitimacy by religious institutions. If the social problem cause has saliency for a person, religiously based endorsement of the cause will enhance the likelihood of the person's moving from bystander or adherent to constituent.

To summarize, secularists and believers alike look for ways to render legitimate the causes they support. Religious legitimacy may not have the taken-for-granted power it did in traditional society, but this by no means renders it impotent in the hearts of individuals and the structures of their institutions. Religious legitimacy is a coveted resource in the struggle to define social problems and press for their resolution. When used skillfully, it can be the decisive resource.

Organization. Three dimensions of organization are pertinent to assessing whether and how a religious institution will become involved in a social problem: (1) organizational strength, (2) structure, and (3) doctrinal-value consensus.

Organizational Strength refers to the position of the institution vis-a-vis reference points external to itself: (1) the total society, (2) the state or government, and (3) other religious groups and reality-defining institutions. Strength in the institution will be reflected in "generalized prestige," the social status of members, and the size of the institution. With respect to the state, the acid test of strength is who, if anyone, in government listens and acts when the religious group speaks. In relation to other religious groups and reality-defining institutions, the record of and potential for cooperation or conflict on social problems, not ideology per se, are key indicators to be assessed.

Calculations of organizational strength reveal not the likelihood of a religious institution's becoming involved in a social problem but, rather, how the institution will become involved and with what consequence. Great strength and organizational consensus likely will lead to behind-the-scenes interest group lobbying efforts; lesser clout will foster social movement activities.

In a series of papers over the past dozen years, James R. Wood has examined the *structural features* of organizations which permit and constrain organizational leaders' participation in social problems. Together these papers provide significant illumination of the organizational dimension of the conceptual model I am advocating. I want to identify several points in his work that are particularly relevant.

To begin, the distinction between hierarchical and congregational authority structures has been made by others, but Wood uses it as a cornerstone to develop empirical evidence explaining how some organizations can protect leaders while others are quite incapable of doing so (Wood, 1970). His concept of *organizational transcendence* helps us understand how organizations and their leaders can move in directions not predictable on the basis of members' values (Wood, 1975). Recently, in collaboration with Hougland, he has provided another piece of the organizational puzzle by demonstrating the effects of size and policy on local congregational control (Hougland and Wood, 1979). In his most recent manuscript, Wood shows how leaders use both *formal* and *attributed legitimacy* to engage in social action reality construction (Wood, 1981). Utilizing the belief structures of the church and drawing upon institutional legitimacy, religious leaders weave general values into specific policy action implications.

In all, Wood has amassed considerable data which illuminate how religious leaders become involved in social problems, and because of this the general state of knowledge about the effects of structure on organizational involvement in social problems is much better developed than are other dimensions. Whereas in other areas the important questions need yet to be identified, this area requires synthesis and the identification of knowledge gaps.

A final pertinent organizational issue in the involvement of a religious institution in a social problem is the matter of *doctrinal-value consensus*. Doctrine refers to a formal belief system; values refer to social beliefs, which may or may not derive from doctrine. Following Wood, we would expect religious leaders to link doctrinal and social values to increase their freedom to engage in social problems causes.

Under conditions of doctrinal consensus, great potential exists for mobilization of manpower to deal with social problems judged to be a threat to the faith. Similarly, consensus about social values will ease involvement. When doctrine and values are linked successfully, response may even be mandated. Consensus across all significant segments of the institution combined with saliency of the issue will produce support for the social problem cause. Contrary to the conclusion I reached regarding the reluctance of many laity to have clergy address social problems (Hadden, 1969), Wood finds laity do not object to clerical involvement in social problems as long as they agree with the position taken (Wood, 1981). Dissensus at any level, however, will produce internal conflict which will in turn affect the institution's effectiveness in dealing with the social problem.

SUMMARY AND CONCLUSIONS

Finally, I shall present a summary of the major ideas developed here and offer a few reflections regarding the practical importance of the central argument.

First, I have tried to identify the relationship between religion and social problems as an important but theoretically underdeveloped area of inquiry. We can locate many scholarly investigations of the religious motivations of individuals who have been involved in the social problem solving arena and even a few studies of particular religious groups. But as an explicit topic of sociological investigation, we lack systematic theory that can be identified as a sociology of religion and social problems.

Second, it is my contention that failure to pursue this topic has resulted, in some considerable measure, from a failure of concepts. On the one hand, we are still struggling to define the basic concepts of our subject matter. On the other, concepts we have accepted and used rather broadly have had beguiling and deflating effects on our sociological imaginations. Chief among these culprits is the concept of secularization. Even those who have questioned its utility have assimilated into their consciousness the underlying message of the concept: the power of religion in modern civilization has been terribly eroded.

I tacitly agree with Collins' (1975:376) conclusion that ''The most important change in political ideologies in the last few hundred years was the decline of religious and the rise of secular ones.'' Having assumed because of our conceptual framework that religion has radically declined in importance in the political arena, we have taken still another cognitive leap and dismissed it as a topic of systematic investigation.

The third point I have tried to present here is a challenge to this traditional sociological theory which, by definition, diminishes the influence of religion in modern consciousness and action. Conceptually, I have argued that the role of religion in defining and dealing with social problems has changed dramatically in the modern secular era. Contrary to the assumption of diminished influence, I have tried to present a case for a much more active role for religion. As carriers of cultural values and ideologies, as well as protectors of their own turf, religious institutions stand in structural tension with the state. They may align, or they may not. The task of a sociology of religion and social problems would be to identify when, why, and how religion and state will be partners or antagonists in the definition of and efforts to resolve social problems.

The final task pursued in this paper has been to identify a conceptual framework wherein we can begin to identify the appropriate questions for developing propositions about religion and social problems. Three issues— interests, resources, and organizational features of religious institutions—were identified as fundamental in analyzing whether, why, and how they would become involved in social problems.

Let me now conclude with an observation, an opinion, a speculation, and a prescription. The *observation* is that religious motivation and religious leaders and institutions have been far more active in the process of defining and giving direction to social problems during this century than we, as social scientists, have recognized. Lewy's (1974) important study, *Religion and Revolution,* reveals quite unmistakenly the potential of all the world's major religions to become involved in struggles to establish a new social-political order. And revolution, after all, is but a special type of social problem-solving activity predicated on the assumption that the reigning political regime is incapable of solving problems.

The *opinion* is that there is a lot of idealistic ferment in this world that seeks avenues of expression. Spanning ideological persuasions from far right to far left, this ferment will find expression under the aegis of the sacred religious canopy. The power of religion to capture this zeal is no less today that it was in the sixteenth century when Richard Hooker eloquently wrote:

persuaded that it is the will of God to have those things done which they fancy, their opinions are as thorns in their sides, never suffering them to take rest till they have brought their speculations into practice (Cited in Lewy, 1974:584).

The *speculation* is that the 1980s will see renewed involvement of religion in the struggle to define and resolve social problems in this nation. If the politically liberal wing of organized religion won the struggle of the 1960s to determine which side God was on, they are by no means assured of triumph in the ensuing struggle. The conservatives are already out of the starting gate and running hard. It is not clear the liberals even know the race is on again. As individuals, many of us feel we have interests involved in the outcome of this intramural contest among religious institutions. Let us join with Joseph Fichter and Paul Furfey in admitting the legitimacy of our own commitments and presuppositions. But in our role as social scientists, it is not our business to care who wins, but to understand how the game is played.

Finally, the *prescription* is this. If we are to understand the variable role of religion in the definition and resolution of social problems, we must jettison our ethnocentric North American bias and begin to pursue comparative cross-cultural studies. To study the role of religion in social problems in America is to investigate only a few frames of a very long film. Recently, religion played a most significant role in toppling two great allies of our Departments of State and Defense in Iran and Nicaragua. Whether these events will work for the betterment of mankind is yet to be determined. Whether the world comes to understand the role of religion in social problems will be determined in considerable measure by whether we accept the challenge to develop theory and research in this important arena.

REFERENCES

Berger, Peter L. 1967. The Sacred Canopy. Garden City, New York: Doubleday.
Collins, Randall. 1975. Conflict Sociology. New York: Academic Press.
Durkheim, Emile. 1965. The Elementary Forms of Religious Life. New York: Free Press. (1912).

Gold, David. 1979. "Social research and social problems: toward a structural explanation of a fuzzy association." *Pacific Sociological Review* 22:275-283.

Hadden, Jeffrey K. 1969. The Gathering Storm in the Churches. Garden City, New York: Doubleday.

Hougland, James G., Jr., and James R. Wood. 1979. "Determinants of organizational control in local churches." *Journal for the Scientific Study of Religion* 18:132-145.

Johnson, Benton. 1963. "On church and sect." *American Sociological Review* 28:535-549.

Lewy, Guenter. 1974. Religion and Revolution. New York: Oxford University Press.

McCarthy, John D., and Mayer N. Zald. 1977. "Resource mobilization and social movements: a partial theory." *American Journal of Sociology* 82:1212-1241.

Spector, Malcolm, and John I. Kitsuse. 1977. Constructing Social Problems. Menlo Park, California: Cummings.

Stark, Rodney, and William Sims Bainbridge. 1979. "Of churches, sects, and cults: preliminary concepts for a theory of religious movements." *Journal for the Scientific Study of Religion* 18:117-131.

Wood, James R. 1970. "Authority and controversial policy: the churches and civil rights." *American Sociological Review* 35:1057-1069.

1975. "Legitimate control and 'organizational transcendence.'" *Social Forces* 54:199-211.

1981. Legitimate Leadership in Voluntary Organizations: The Controversy Over Social Action in Protestant Churches. Brunswick, N.J.: Rutgers Univ. Press.

II
New Religions

$\mathbf{T}$HERE has been no more vivid manifestation of religion's new relevance than the almost frantic creation and adoption of new gods during the 1970s. As late as 1970, when *Sociological Analysis* reviewed trends in the study of religion, sects and cults were only curiosities on the deviant fringe of religious activity. Questions about the future of established religion in an increasingly secular society seemed far more important then. While scholars were preoccupied with those problems, though, the youth counterculture of the 1960s had spawned a plethora of new religions. By their visible disregard for conventional values and their hostility to established institutions, these movements rapidly gained notoriety of their own. Moonie "brainwashing," the Jonestown murder/suicides, Scientology's battle with the FBI, deprogramming and similar events put religion back in the headlines. The ensuing controversy over cults rejuvenated consciousness of religion, if not religious consciousness, among those who had given up religion for dead, including many scholars.

The headlines attracted scholars and journalists in waves. By the end of the 1970s, the literature on new religious movements had swelled so greatly there appeared to be hardly anything left to say about them. The three papers collected here testify to the contrary. Looking behind the headlines, each of them takes up a basic sociological issue neglected in the rush to keep abreast of those startling events. Bainbridge and Stark consider how cults get started, Bird how they affect moral consciousness, and Shupe and Bromley how people react to them. By focusing our attention on issues of enduring significance for society and for scholarship, they help bring the study of new religions to maturity.

Bainbridge and Stark contribute to that end by sifting the great mass of ethnographic information on cults for clues to their social origins ("Cult Formation: Three Compatible Models"). Most explanations center on the *psychopathology* of the cult founder, and there is considerable empirical support for that thesis. In addition, though, these scholars also find evidence for what they call the *entrepreneurial* and *sub-cultural-evolutionary* explanations, each of which they sketch here for the first time. The former suggests that cults originate in efforts to capitalize on the market for cultic magic, which leads enterprising members of successful cults to split off and form their own groups. The latter sees religion emerging as a byproduct of intensive social relations within groups trying unsuccessfully to accomplish something else of value to them. Those two models complement the psychopathology explanations by uncovering the roots of cult formation in the contingencies of ordinary life. Together, the three models provide a much stronger basis for understanding the genesis of new religions than psychopathology alone.

In his paper on cults and moral accountability ("The Pursuit of Innocence") Frederick Bird reconsiders a classic issue in contemporary context. We have traditionally assumed that religious commitment binds people more strongly to the moral order, but Bird shows that cult religion today tends to *reduce the individual sense of moral accountability*. Beginning with initiation, which is Bird's focus here, new religions impress upon the convert a relation to the sacred, a structure of authority and a moral model which diminishes the sense of accountability, though in slightly different ways depending on the type of group. This unlikely pattern, he suggests, arises from the modern dilemma of moral accountability organized by the persistent demands of institutional norms in an era which glorifies personal liberation from those norms. By showing that the historical context of religion shapes its moral relevance in unanticipated ways, he calls us to rethink some of our most basic assumptions.

It is rare for scholars to gain entrée to conflicting groups, but David Bromley and Anson Shupe accomplished it in their studies of the Unification Church and its adversaries. Here ("Moonies and the Anti-Cultists") they use the resource mobilization perspective on social movements to analyze the anti-cult movement. They show how the hostile reaction to Moonies arose from the family and established religion in response to the threat of "world transformation" by the cultists. The perceived threat to families generated intense activity focused on very specific goals (e.g., rescuing their own children), but its very success in those endeavors seriously limited the possibilities of sustaining a coherent and powerful general movement at the national level.

2

CULT FORMATION:
THREE COMPATIBLE MODELS

William Sims Bainbridge, Rodney Stark

The origins of the great world faiths are shrouded by time, but cult formation remains available for close inspection. If we would understand how religions begin, it is the obscure and exotic world of cults that demands our attention. This paper attempts to synthesize the mass of ethnographic materials available on cult formation as the necessary preliminary for a comprehensive theory. While it represents an important step in our continuing work to formulate a general theory of religion, this paper is primarily designed to consolidate and to clarify what is already known about this subject.

The published literature on cults is at present as chaotic as was the material on which cultural anthropology was founded a century ago: an unsystematic collection of traveler's tales, mostly journalistic, often inaccurate, and nearly devoid of theory. For all the deficiencies of this mass of writing, three fundamental models of how novel religious ideas are generated and made social can be seen dimly. In this paper we develop and compare these models. The task of integrating them fully into a single, comprehensive theory must be delayed, but in this first exposition we will be able to show that each model is but a different combination of the same theoretical elements.

The three models of cult formation, or religious innovation, are (a) *the psychopathology model*, (b) *the entrepreneur model,* and (c) *the subculture-evolution model*. While the first has been presented in some detail by other social scientists, the second and third have not previously been delineated as formal models.

Cult formation is a two-step process of innovation. First, new religious ideas must be *invented*. Second, *social acceptance* of these ideas must be gained, at least to the extent that a small group of people comes to accept them. Therefore, our first need is to explain how and why individuals invent or discover new religious ideas. It is important to recognize, however, that many (perhaps most) persons who hit upon new religious ideas do not found new religions. So long as only one person holds a religious idea, no true religion exists. Therefore, we also need to understand the process by which religious inventors are able to make their views social—to convince other persons to share their convictions. We conceptualize successful cult innovation as a social process in which innovators both invent new religious ideas and transmit them to other persons in exchange for rewards.

RELIGIONS AS EXCHANGE SYSTEMS

Human action is governed by the pursuit of rewards and the avoidance of costs. Rewards, those things humans will expend costs to obtain, often can be gained only from other humans, so people are forced into exchange relations. However, many rewards are very scarce and can only be possessed by some, not all. Some rewards appear to be so scarce that they cannot be shown to exist at all. For example, people act as if eternal life were a reward of immense value. But there is no *empirical* evidence that such a reward can be gained at any price. From these basic observations, we are developing a general theory of religion (Stark and Bainbridge, 1979; 1980). Our key concept is that of *compensators*.

Faced with rewards that are very scarce, or not available at all, humans create and exchange compensators—sets of beliefs and prescriptions for action that substitute for the immediate achievement of the desired reward. Compensators postulate the attainment of the desired reward in the distant future or in some other unverifiable context. Compensators are treated by humans as if they were rewards. They have the character of IOUs, the value of which must be taken on faith. Promises that the poor will be rich following the revolution or that the mortal will be immortal in another world are such compensators.

Just as rewards differ in the value accorded them by humans, so do compensators. Furthermore, compensators vary in the extent to which they are specific (substituting for specific, limited rewards of moderate value) or general (substituting for a great number of highly desired rewards). A magical "cure" for headaches is a specific compensator, while Heaven is the most general compensator, promising an unlimited stream of future rewards to those humans fortunate or virtuous enough to be admitted. Relatively specific compensators are offered by many kinds of secular institutions, as well as by religion, while the most general compensators seem to require the supernatural agencies postulated by religious doctrines.

We define religions as social enterprises whose primary purpose is to create, maintain, and exchange supernaturally-based general compensators (Stark and Bainbridge, 1979). We thus eliminate from the definition many non-supernatural sources of compensators, such as political movements. We also exclude magic, which deals only in quite specific compensators and does not offer compensators on the grand scale of Heaven or of religious doctrines about the meaning of life (Cf. Durkheim, 1915).

We define cults as social enterprises primarily engaged in the production and exchange of novel and exotic compensators. Thus not all cults are religions. Some cults offer only magic, for example psychic healing of specific diseases, and do not offer such *general* compensators as eternal life. Magical cults frequently evolve toward more general compensators and become full-fledged religions. They then become true *cult movements:* social enterprises primarily engaged in the production and exchange of novel and exotic general compensators based on supernatural assumptions.

Often a cult is exotic and offers compensators that are unfamiliar to most people because it migrated from another, alien society. Here we are not interested in these *imported cults* but in those novel cult movements that are innovative alternatives to the traditional systems of religious compensators that are normal in the environment in which the cult originated.

Having briefly described our theoretical perspective and defined key concepts, we are now ready to understand the three models of cult innovation and to see their common propositions.

THE PSYCHOPATHOLOGY MODEL OF CULT INNOVATION

The *psychopathology model* has been used by many anthropologists and ethnopsychiatrists, and it is related closely to deprivation theories of revolutions and social movements (Smelser, 1962; Gurr, 1970). It describes cult innovation as the result of individual psychopathology that finds successful social expression. Because of its popularity among social scientists, this model exists in many variants, but the main ideas are the following.

1. Cults are novel cultural responses to personal and societal crisis.

2. New cults are invented by individuals suffering from certain forms of mental illness.

3. These individuals typically achieve their novel visions during psychotic episodes.

4. During such an episode, the individual invents a new package of compensators to meet his own needs.

5. The individual's illness commits him to his new vision, either because his hallucinations appear to demonstrate its truth, or because his compelling needs demand immediate satisfaction.

6. After the episode, the individual will be most likely to succeed in forming a cult around his vision if the society contains many other persons

suffering from problems similar to those originally faced by the cult founder, to whose solution, therefore, they are likely to respond.

7. Therefore, such cults most often succeed during times of societal crisis, when large numbers of persons suffer from similar unresolved problems.

8. If the cult does succeed in attracting many followers, the individual founder may achieve at least a partial cure of his illness, because his self-generated compensators are legitimated by other persons, and because he now receives true rewards from his followers.

The psychopathology model is supported by the traditional psychoanalytic view that magic and religion are mere projections of neurotic wish-fulfillment or psychotic delusions (Freud, 1927, 1930; Roheim, 1955; La Barre, 1969, 1972). However, the model does not assume that cultic ideas are necessarily wrong or insane. Rather, it addresses the question of how individuals can invent deviant perspectives and then have conviction in them, despite the lack of objective, confirmatory evidence.

All societies provide traditional compensator-systems which are familiar to all members of the society and which have considerable plausibility, both because their assumptions are familiar and because of the numbers of people already committed to them. Why, then, would some persons reject the conventional religious tradition, concoct apparently arbitrary substitutes, and put their trust in these novel formulations? The psychopathology model notes that highly neurotic or psychotic persons typically do just this, whether in a religious framework or not. By definition, the mentally ill are mentally deviant. Furthermore, especially in the case of psychotics, they mistake the products of their own minds for external realities. Thus their pathology provides them not only with abnormal ideas, but also with subjective evidence for the correctness of their ideas, whether in the form of hallucinations or in the form of pressing needs which cannot be denied.

A number of authors have identified occult behavior with specific psychiatric syndromes. Hysteria frequently has been blamed. Cult founders often do suffer from apparent physical illness, find a spiritual "cure" for their own ailment, then dramatize that cure as the basis of the cult performance (Messing, 1958; Lévi-Strauss, 1963; Lewis, 1971). A well-known American example is Mary Baker Eddy, whose invention of Christian Science apparently was a successful personal response to a classic case of hysteria (Zweig, 1932).

In other cases a manic-depressive pattern is found. John Humphrey Noyes, founder of the Oneida community, had an obsessive need to be "perfect," and in his more elevated periods was able to convince a few dozen people that he had indeed achieved perfection and that he could help them attain this happy state as well. But the times of elation were followed by "eternal spins," depressive states in which Noyes was immobilized by self-hatred (Carden, 1969).

Classical paranoia and paranoid schizophrenia also have been blamed for producing cults. A person who founds a cult asserts the arrogant claim that he (above all others) has achieved a miraculous cultural breakthrough, a claim that outsiders may perceive as a delusion of grandeur. For example, L. Ron Hubbard announced his invention of Dianetics (later to become Scientology) by saying that "the creation of dianetics is a milestone for Man comparable to his discovery of fire and superior to his inventions of the wheel and arch" (Hubbard, 1950).

Martin Gardner has shown that the position of the cultist or pseudoscientist in his social environment is nearly identical to that of the clinical paranoid. Neither is accorded the high social status he demands from conventional authorities and is contemptuously ignored by societal leaders or harshly persecuted. Gardner notes that paranoia actually may be an advantage under these circumstances because without it the individual "would lack the stamina to fight a vigorous, single-handed battle against such overwhelming odds" (Gardner, 1957).

Many biographies of cult founders contain information that would support any of these diagnoses, and often the syndrome appears to be a life pattern that antedated the foundation of the cult by a number of years. However, the symptoms of these disorders are so close to the features that *define* cult activity that simplistic psychopathology explanations approach tautology. Lemert (1967) has argued that social exclusion and conflict over social status can *produce* the symptoms of paranoia. It may be that some cult founders display symptoms of mental illness as a *result* of societal rejection of their cults. Another problem faced by the psychopathology model is the fact that the vast majority of mental patients have not founded cults.

The simplest version of the model states that the founder's psychopathology had a physiological cause. Religious visions may appear during psychotic episodes induced by injury, drugs, and high fevers. If an episode takes place outside any medical setting, the individual may find a supernatural explanation of his experience most satisfactory (Sargant, 1959). Innumerable examples exist. Love Israel, founder of a cult called The Love Family, told us that his religious vision was triggered by hallucinogenic drugs which enabled him to experience a state of fusion with another man who subsequently became a prominent follower. The stories of some persons who claim to have been contacted by flying saucers sound very much like brief episodes of brain disorder to which the individual has retrospectively given a more favorable interpretation (Greenberg, 1979).

More subtle variants of the psychopathology model present psychodynamic explanations and place the process of cult formation in a social context. Julian Silverman (1967) outlined a five-step model describing the early career of a *shaman* (sorcerer, witch doctor, magical healer) or cult founder. In the first stage, the individual is beset by a serious personal and social problem, typically severely damaged self-esteem, that defies practical solution. In the second stage, the individual becomes preoccupied with his problem and withdraws from active social life. Some cultures even have formalized rituals of withdrawal in which the individual may leave the settlement and dwell temporarily in the wilderness. The Bible abounds in examples of withdrawal to the wilderness to prepare for a career as a prophet. This immediately leads to the third stage in which the individual experiences "self-initiated sensory deprivation," which can produce very extreme psychotic symptoms even in previously normal persons. Thus begins the fourth stage, in which the future cult founder receives his supernatural vision. "What follows then is the eruption into the field of attention of a flood of archaic imagery and attendant lower-order referential processes such as occur in dreams or reverie .... Ideas surge through with peculiar vividness as though from an outside source" (Silverman, 1967:28). In the fifth stage, *cognitive reorganization,* the individual attempts to share his vision with other people. If he fails, he lapses into chronic mental illness, but if he finds social support for his supernatural claims, he can become a successful shaman or cult leader. If his followers reward him sufficiently with honor, the originally damaged self-esteem that provoked the entire sequence will be repaired completely, and the cult founder may even become one of the best-adapted members of his social group.

The theory of revitalization movements proposed by Anthony F.C. Wallace (1956) is similar to Silverman's model but adds the important ingredient of social crisis. Wallace suggests that a variety of threats to a society can produce greatly increased stress on members: "climatic, floral and faunal change; military defeat; political subordination; extreme pressure toward acculturation resulting in internal cultural conflict; economic distress; epidemics; and so on" (Wallace, 1956:269). Under stress, some individuals begin to go through the process outlined by Silverman, and under favorable circumstances, they achieve valuable cultural reformulations which they can use as the basis of social action to revitalize their society. While Wallace advocates a pure form of the psychopathology model, he concludes "that the religious vision experience per se is not psychopathological but rather the reverse, being a synthesizing and often therapeutic process performed under extreme stress by individuals already sick" (Wallace, 1956:273).

The importance of the psychopathology model is underscored by Wallace's suggestion that many historically influential social movements, and perhaps *all major religions,* originated according to its principles. This view is held by Weston La Barre (1972) who says that every religion without exception originated as a "crisis cult," using this term for cults that emerge according to the pattern described by Wallace. Among many examples, he specifically describes even Christianity as a typical crisis cult. Writing in an orthodox Freudian tradition, La Barre identifies the source of a cult founder's vision: "A god is only a shaman's dream about his father" (La Barre, 1972:19). He says the shaman is an immature man who desperately needs compensation for his inadequacies, including sexual incapacity, and in finding magical compensations for himself, he generates compensators for use by more normal persons as well (La Barre, 1972:138).

Claude Lévi-Strauss, an exchange theorist as well as a structuralist, emphasizes that the shaman participates in an economy of meaning. Normal persons want many kinds of rewards they cannot obtain and can be convinced to accept compensators generated by fellow citizens less tied to reality than they. "In a universe which it strives to understand but whose dynamics it cannot fully control, normal thought continually seeks the meaning of things which refuse to reveal their significance. So-called pathological thought, on the other hand, overflows with emotional interpretations and overtones, in order to supplement an otherwise deficient reality" (Lévi-Strauss, 1963:175). In shamanism, the neurotic producer of compensators and the suffering normal consumer come together in an exchange beneficial to both, participating in the exchange of compensators for tangible rewards that is the basis of all cults.

THE ENTREPRENEUR MODEL OF CULT INNOVATION

The *entrepreneur model* of cult innovation has not received as much attention from social scientists as the *psychopathology model.* We have known for decades that the psychopathology model could not explain adequately all cultic phenomena (Ackerknecht, 1943), but attempts to construct alternate models have been desultory. Of course, it is difficult to prove that any given cult founder was psychologically normal, but in many cases even rather lengthy biographies fail to reveal significant evidence of pathology. While the psychopathology model focuses on cult founders who invent new compensator-systems initially for their own use, the entrepreneur model notes that cult founders often may *consciously develop new compensator-systems in order to exchange them for great rewards.* Innovation pays off in many other areas of culture, such as technological invention and artistic creativity. If social circumstances provide opportunities for profit in the field of cults, then many perfectly normal individuals will be attracted to the challenge.

Models of entrepreneurship have been proposed to explain many other kinds of human activity, but we have not found adequate social-scientific models specifically designed to explain cult innovation. Journalists have documented that such a model would apply well to many cases, and our own observations in several cults amply confirm that conclusion. Therefore, we shall sketch the beginnings of an entrepreneur model, with the understanding that much future work will be required before this analytic approach is fully developed. The chief ideas of such a model might be the following.

1. Cults are businesses which provide a product for their customers and receive payment in return.

2. Cults are mainly in the business of selling novel compensators, or at least freshly packaged compensators that appear new.

3. Therefore, a supply of novel compensators must be manufactured.

4. Both manufacture and sales are accomplished by entrepreneurs.

5. These entrepreneurs, like those in other businesses, are motivated by the desire for profit, which they can gain by exchanging compensators for rewards.

6. Motivation to enter the cult business is stimulated by the perception that such business can be profitable, an impression likely to be acquired through prior involvement with a successful cult.

7. Successful entrepreneurs require skills and experience, which are most easily gained through a prior career as the employee of an earlier successful cult.

8. The manufacture of salable new compensators (or compensator-packages) is most easily accomplished by assembling components of pre-existing compensator-systems into new configurations, or by the further development of successful compensator-systems.

9. Therefore, cults tend to cluster in lineages. They are linked by individual entrepreneurs who begin their careers in one cult and then leave to found their own. They bear strong "family resemblances" because they share many cultural features.

10. Ideas for completely new compensators can come from any cultural source or personal experience whatsoever, but the skillful entrepreneur experiments carefully in the development of new products and incorporates them permanently in his cult only if the market response is favorable.

Cults can in fact be very successful businesses. The secrecy that surrounds many of these organizations prevents us from reporting current financial statistics, but a few figures have been revealed. Arthur L. Bell's cult, Mankind United, received contributions totalling four million dollars in the ten years preceeding 1944 (Dohrman, 1958:41). In the four years 1956-1959, the Washington, D.C., branch of Scientology took in $758,982 and gave its founder, L. Ron Hubbard, $100,000 plus the use of a home and car (Cooper, 1971:109). Today Scientology has many flourishing branches, and Hubbard lives on his own 320-foot ship. In 1973 a small cult we have called The Power was grossing $100,000 a month, four thousand of this going directly to the husband and wife team who ran the operation from their comfortable Westchester County estate (Bainbridge, 1978). In addition to obvious material benefits, successful cult founders also receive intangible but valuable rewards, including praise, power, and amusement. Many cult leaders have enjoyed almost unlimited sexual access to attractive followers (Orrmont, 1961; Carden, 1969).

The simplest variant of the entrepreneur model, and the one preferred by journalists, holds that cult innovators are outright frauds who have no faith in their own product and sell it through trickery to fools and desperate persons. We have many examples of cults that were pure confidence games, and we shall mention examples of fraud in three kinds of cult: audience cults, client cults, and cult movements.

Audience cults offer very specific and weak compensators, often no more than a mild, vicarious thrill or entertainment, and they lack both long-term clients and formal membership. *Client cults* offer valued but relatively specific compensators, frequently alleged cures for particular diseases and emotional problems, and they may possess a relatively stable clientele without counting them as full members of the organization. *Cult movements* deal in a much more elaborate package of compensators, including the most general compensators based on supernatural assumptions, and they possess committed membership. In terms of their compensators, these three levels of cults can be described conveniently in traditional language: Audience cults provide *mythology;* client cults add serious *magic;* cult movements give complete *religion.*

In 1973, Israeli prestidigitator Uri Geller barnstormed the United States presenting himself as a psychic who could read minds and bend spoons by sheer force of will. As James Randi (1975) has shown, Geller's feats were achieved through trickery, and yet untold thousands of people were fascinated by the possibility that Geller might have real psychic powers. The whole affair was a grand but short-lived audience cult.

Medical client cults based on intentional fraud are quite common. A number of con artists not only have discovered that they can use the religious label to appeal to certain kinds of gullible marks, but also have learned that the label provides a measure of protection against legal prosecution (Glick and Newsom, 1974). In many of these cases it may be impossible to prove whether the cult founder was sincere or not, and we can only assume that many undetected frauds lurk behind a variety of client cults. In some cases the trickery is so blatant that we can have little doubt. Among the most recent examples are the Philippine psychic surgeons Terte and Agpaoa, and their Brasilian colleague, Arigo. These men perform fake surgery with their bare hands or brandishing crude jackknives. In some cases they may actually pierce the patient's skin, but often they merely pretend to do so and then spread animal gore about to simulate the results of deep cutting. Through a skillful performance they convince their patients not only that dangerous tumors have been removed from their bodies, but also that the surgeon's psychic powers have instantaneously healed the wound. But their failure actually to perform real operations in this manner must be clear to the psychic surgeons themselves (Flammonde, 1975).

Arthur L. Bell's cult movement was a fraud based on the traditional Rosicrucian idea that a vast benevolent conspiracy prepares to rule the world and invites a few ordinary people to join its elite ranks. Bell claimed only to be the Superintendent of the Pacific Coast Division, in constant communication with his superiors in the (fictitious) organizational hierarchy. In this way he was able to convince his followers that they were members of an immensely powerful secret society, despite the fact that the portion of it they could see was modest in size. Like several similar fraudulent movements, Bell's cult did not originally claim religious status, but only became a "church" after encountering legal difficulty (Dohrman, 1958).

In order to grow, a cult movement must serve real religious functions for its committed followers, regardless of the private intentions of the founder. Many older cults probably were frauds in origin, but have been transformed into genuine religious organizations by followers who deeply believed the founder's deceptions.

But fraud need not be involved in entrepreneurial cult innovation. Many ordinary businessmen are convinced of the value of their products by the fact that customers want to buy them, and cult entrepreneurs may likewise accept their market as the ultimate standard of value. Many cult founders do appear to be convinced by testimonials from satisfied customers that their compensator-packages are valuable. This was probably the case with Franz Anton Mesmer, who saw astonishing transformations in his clients, apparently the beneficial results of his techniques, and who found in them ample evidence of the truth of his theories (Zweig, 1932; Darnton, 1970). Practitioners of all client cults frequently see similar evidence in favor of their own ideas, no matter how illogical, because all such cults provide compensators of at least some strength (Frank, 1963).

Another source of confidence for the cult innovator is his experience with other cults. Early in their careers, innovators typically join one or more successful cults, and honestly may value the cults' products themselves.

However, the innovator may be dissatisfied with the older cults and come to the sincere opinion that he can create a more satisfactory product. Despite their often intense competition, cult leaders frequently express respect and admiration for other cults, including the ones with which they themselves were previously associated. For example, L. Ron Hubbard of Scientology has praised Alfred Korzybski's General Semantics, and Jack Horner of Dianology has praised Hubbard's Scientology.

Once we realize that cult formation often involves entrepreneurial action to establish a profitable new organization based on novel culture, we can see that concepts developed to understand technological innovation should apply here as well. For example, a study of entrepreneurship and technology by Edward B. Roberts (1969) examined the cultural impact of the Massachusetts Institute of Technology, the preeminent center of new technological culture. Over 200 new high-technology companies had been founded by former M.I.T. employees who concluded they could achieve greater personal rewards by establishing their own businesses based on what they had learned at M.I.T. The current cult equivalent of M.I.T. is Scientology, studied by one of us in 1970. Cultic entrepreneurs have left Scientology to found countless other cults based on modified Scientology ideas, including Jack Horner's Dianology, H. Charles Berner's Abilitism, Harold Thompson's Amprinistics, and the flying saucer cult described in the ethnography *When Prophecy Fails* (Festinger *et al.,* 1956). Scientology, like M.I.T., is a vast storehouse of exotic culture derived from many sources. Social scientists studying patterns of cultural development should be aware that an occasional key organization can be an influential nexus of innovation and diffusion.

Future research can determine the most common processes through which entrepreneurial cult founders actually invent their novel ideas. We suspect the main techniques involve the cultural equivalent of recombinant DNA genetic engineering. Essentially, the innovator takes the cultural configuration of an existing cult, removes some components, and replaces them with other components taken from other sources. Often, the innovator may simply splice pieces of two earlier cults together. In some cases, the innovator preserves the supporting skeleton of practices and basic assumptions of a cult he admires, and merely grafts on new symbolic flesh. Rosicrucianism affords a sequence of many connected examples (McIntosh, 1972; King, 1970). In creating the AMORC Rosicrucian order, H. Spencer Lewis took European Rosicrucian principles of the turn of the century, including the hierarchical social structure of an initiatory secret society, and grafted on a veneer of symbolism taken from Ancient Egypt, thus capitalizing on public enthusiasm for Egyptian civilization current at that time. His headquarters in San José, California, is a city block of simulated Egyptian buildings. Later, Rose Dawn imitated Lewis in creating her rival Order of the Ancient Mayans. In great measure, she simply replaced AMORC's symbols with equivalent symbols. Instead of Lewis' green biweekly mail-order lessons emblazoned with Egyptian architecture and Egyptian hieroglyphics, she sold red biweekly mail-order lessons decorated with Mayan architecture and Mayan hieroglyphics.

The highly successful EST cult is derived partly from Scientology and well illustrates the commercialism of many such organizations in contemporary America. Werner Erhard, founder of EST, had some experience with Scientology in 1969. Later, he worked for a while in Mind Dynamics, itself an offshoot of José Silva's Mind Control. After Erhard started his own cult in 1971, he decided to emulate Scientology's tremendous success and hired two Scientologists to adapt its practices for his own use. We should note that conventional businesses, such as auto companies and television networks, often imitate each other in pursuit of profit. Erhard's research and development efforts were rewarded, and by the beginning of 1976, an estimated seventy thousand persons had completed his $250 initial seminar (Kornbluth, 1976).

We suggest that cult entrepreneurs will imitate those features of other successful cults which seem to them most responsible for success. They will innovate either in non-essential areas or in areas where they believe they can increase the salability of the product. In establishing their own cult businesses they must innovate at least superficially. They cannot seize a significant part of the market unless they achieve product differentiation. Otherwise they will be at a great disadvantage in direct competition with the older, more prosperous cult on which theirs is patterened. The apparent novelty of a cult's compensator-package may be a sales advantage when the public has not yet discovered the limitations of the rewards that members actually will receive in the new cult and when older compensator-packages have been discredited to some extent. Much research and theory-building remains to be done, but the insight that cults often are examples of skillful free enterprise immediately explains many of the features of the competitive world of cults.

THE SUBCULTURE–EVOLUTION MODEL OF CULT INNOVATION

While the *psychopathology* and *entrepreneur* models stress the role of the individual innovator, the *subculture-evolution model* emphasizes group interaction processes. It suggests that cults can emerge without authoritative leaders, and it points out that even radical cultural developments can be achieved through many small steps. Although much social-psychological literature would be useful in developing this model, we are not aware of a comprehensive statement on cult innovation through subcultural evolution, so again we will attempt to outline the model ourselves.

1. Cults are the expression of novel social systems, usually small in size but composed of at least a few intimately interacting individuals.

2. These cultic social systems are most likely to emerge in populations already deeply involved in the occult milieu, but cult evolution may also begin in entirely secular settings.

3. Cults are the result of sidetracked or failed collective attempts to obtain scarce or nonexistent rewards.

4. The evolution begins when a group of persons commits itself to the attainment of certain rewards.

5. In working together to obtain these rewards, members begin exchanging other rewards as well, such as affect.

6. As they progressively come to experience failure in achieving their original goals, they will gradually generate and exchange compensators as well.

7. If the intragroup exchange of rewards and compensators becomes sufficiently intense, the group will become relatively encapsulated, in the extreme case undergoing complete social implosion.

8. Once separated to some degree from external control, the evolving cult develops and consolidates a novel culture, energized by the need to facilitate the exchange of rewards and compensators, and inspired by essentially accidental factors.

9. The end point of successful cult evolution is a novel religious culture embodied in a distinct social group which must now cope with the problem of extracting resources (including new members) from the surrounding environment.

In writing about juvenile delinquency, Albert K. Cohen (1955) described the process of *mutual conversion* through which interacting individuals could gradually create a deviant normative structure. This process may result in criminal behavior, but it may also result in the stimulation of unrealizable hopes and of faith in the promise of impossible rewards. Thus, *mutual conversion* can describe the social process through which people progressively commit each other to a package of compensators which they simultaneously assemble. It begins when people with similar needs and desires meet and begin communicating about their mutual problems. It takes place in tiny, even imperceptible exploratory steps, as one individual expresses a hope or a plan and receives positive feedback in the form of similar hopes and plans from his fellows. "The final product ... is likely to be a compromise formation of all the participants to what we may call a cultural process, a formation perhaps unanticipated by any of them. Each actor may contribute something directly to the growing product, but he may also contribute indirectly by encouraging others to advance, inducing them to retreat, and suggesting new avenues to be explored. The product cannot be ascribed to any one of the participants; it is a real 'emergent' on a group level'' (Cohen, 1955:60).

Cohen says all human action "is an ongoing series of efforts to solve problems" (1955:50). All human beings face the problem of coping with frustration because some highly desired rewards, such as everlasting life, do not exist in this world. Through mutual conversion, individuals band together to solve one or more shared problems, and the outcome presumably depends on a number of factors, including the nature of the problems and the group's initial conceptualization of them. We suspect a cultic solution is most likely if the people begin by attempting to improve themselves (as in psychotherapy) or to improve their relationship to the natural world, and then fail in their efforts. Criminal or political outcomes are more likely if people believe that other persons or social conditions are responsible for their problems.

The quest for unavailable rewards is not reserved for poor and downtrodden folk alone. Many elite social movements have been dedicated to the attainment of goals that ultimately proved unattainable. One well-documented example is The Committee for the Future, an institutionally detached little organization that formed within the network of technological social movements oriented toward spaceflight. Founded in 1970 by a wealthy couple, the CFF was dedicated to the immediate colonization of the moon and planets and to beginning a new age in which the field of man's activity would be the entire universe. The biggest effort of the CFF, Project Harvest Moon, was intended to establish the first demonstration colony on the moon, planted using a surplus Saturn V launch vehicle. Ultimately, high cost and questionable feasibility prevented any practical accomplishments. In struggling to arouse public support, the CFF held a series of open conventions at which participants collectively developed grand schemes for a better world. Blocked from any success in this direction, the CFF evolved toward cultism. The convention seminars became encounter groups. Mysticism and parapsychology replaced spaceflight as the topic of conversation. Rituals of psychic fusion were enacted to religious music, and the previously friendly aerospace companies and agencies broke off with the Committee. Denied success in its original purposes, and unfettered by strong ties to conventional institutions, the CFF turned ever more strongly toward compensators and toward the supernatural (Bainbridge, 1976).

Cults are particularly likely to emerge wherever numbers of people seek help for intractable personal problems. The broad fields of psychotherapy, rehabilitation, and personal development have been especially fertile for cults. A number of psychotherapy services have evolved into cult movements, including those created by some of Freud's immediate followers (Rieff, 1968). Other independent human service organizations may also be susceptible to cultic evolution. The best-known residential program designed to treat drug addiction, Synanon, has recently evolved into an authoritarian cult movement that recruits persons who never suffered from drug problems.

Two important factors render cultic evolution more likely. First, the process will progress most easily if there are no binding external constraints. For example, psychiatrists and psychologists who work in institutional settings (such as hospitals or universities) may be prevented by their conventional commitments from participating in the evolution of a cult, while independent practitioners are more free. Second, the process will be facilitated if the therapist *receives* compensators as well as gives them and thus participates fully in the inflation and proliferation of compensators.

A good example is The Power, founded in London in 1963, which began as an independent psychotherapy service designed to help normal individuals achieve supernormal levels of functioning. The therapy was based on Alfred Adler's theory that each human being is impelled by subconscious *goals,* and it attempted to bring these goals to consciousness so the person could pursue them more effectively and escape inner conflict. The founders of The Power received the therapy as well as gave it, and frequent group sessions brought all participants together to serve each other's emotional needs. The Power recruited clients through the founders' pre-existing friendship network, and the therapy sessions greatly intensified the strength and intimacy of their social bonds.

As bonds strengthened, the social network became more thoroughly interconnected as previously distant persons were brought together. The rudiments of a group culture evolved, and many individuals contributed ideas about how the therapy might be improved and expanded. Participants came to feel that only other participants understood them completely, and found communication with outsiders progressively more difficult. A *social implosion* took place.

In a social implosion, part of an extended social network collapses as social ties within it strengthen and, reciprocally, those to persons outside it weaken. It is a step-by-step process. Social implosions may be set off by more than one circumstance. In the case of The Power, the implosion was initiated by the introduction of a new element of culture, a "therapy" technique that increased the intimacy of relations around a point in the network. Correlated with the implosion was a mutual conversion as members encouraged each other to express their deepest fantasies and to believe they could be fulfilled. The Adlerian analysis of subconscious goals was ideally designed to arouse longings and hopes for all the unobtained and unobtainable rewards the participants had ever privately wished to receive. The powerful affect and social involvement produced by the implosion were tangible rewards that convinced participants that the other rewards soon would be achieved. Concomitant estrangement from outside attachments led The Power to escape London to the isolation of a ruined seaside Yucatan plantation. Remote from the restraining influence of conventional society, The Power completed its evolution from psychotherapy to religion by inventing supernatural doctrines to explain how its impossible, absolute goals might ultimately be achieved. When the new cult returned to civilization in 1967, it became legally incorporated as a church (Bainbridge, 1978).

Since non-religious groups can evolve into religious cults, it is not surprising that cults also can arise from religious sects—extreme religious groups that accept the standard religious tradition of the society, unlike cults that are revolutionary breaks with the culture of past churches. An infamous example is The People's Temple of Jim Jones that destroyed itself in the jungles of Guyana. This group began as an emotionally extreme but culturally traditional Christian sect, then evolved into a cult as Jones progressively became a prophet with an ever more radical vision. Of course, either the psychopathology or entrepreneur models may apply in this case. But the committed members of the sect probably contributed to the transformation by encouraging Jones step-by-step, and by demanding of him the accomplishment of impossible goals. Even when a single individual dominates a group, the subculture-evolution model will apply to the extent that the followers also participate in pushing the group toward cultism. In this case, the needs of the followers and their social relationships with the leader may have served as a *psychopathology amplifier*, reflecting back to Jones his own narcissism multiplied by the strength of their unreasonable hopes.

CONCLUSION

Each of the three models identifies a system of production and exchange of compensators. In the *psychopathology model,* a cult founder creates compensators initially for his own use, then gives them followers in return for rewards. In the *entrepreneur model,* the cult founder sets out to gain rewards by manufacturing compensators intended for sale to followers. The *subculture-evolution model* describes the interplay of many individual actions in which various individuals at different times play the roles of producer and consumer of novel compensators.

While the models may appear to compete, in fact they complement each other and can be combined to explain the emergence of particular cults. After a cult founder has escaped a period of psychopathology, he may act as an entrepreneur in promoting or improving his cult. An entrepreneur threatened with loss of his cult may be driven into an episode of psychopathology that provides new visions that contribute to a new success. The subculture-evolution model may include many little episodes of psychopathology and entrepreneurial enterprise participated in by various members, woven together by a complex network of social exchanges.

Taken together, the psychopathology, entrepreneur and subculture-evolution models foreshadow a general theory of cult innovation that can be constructed using their elements connected logically within the framework of exchange theory. They offer numerous explanatory hypotheses that could be tested using the store of historical information found in any large library or using new data collected in future field research. The models also provide a checklist of important questions to guide the ethnographer in performing the study of a cult. Until now, the social science of cult innovation has lacked a clear body of theory and a research program. The three models developed in this paper provide a solid basis for studying the emergence of new religions.

REFERENCES

Ackerknecht, Erwin H. 1943. "Psychopathology, primitive medicine and primitive culture." *Bulletin of the History of Medicine* 14:30-67.

Bainbridge, William Sims. 1976. The Spaceflight Revolution. New York: Wiley.

1978. Satan's Power. Berkeley: University of California.

Bainbridge, William Sims, and Rodney Stark. 1980. "Sectarian tension." *Review of Religious Research* 22:105-24.

Carden, Maren Lockwood. 1969. Oneida: Utopian Community to Modern Corporation. Baltimore: Johns Hopkins.

Cohen, Albert K. 1955. Delinquent Boys. New York: Free Press.

Cooper, Paulette. 1971. The Scandal of Scientology. New York: Tower.

Darnton, Robert. 1970. Mesmerism and the End of the Enlightenment in France. New York: Schocken.

Dohrman, H.T. 1958. California Cult. Boston: Beacon.

Durkheim, Emile. 1915. The Elementary Forms of the Religious Life. London: Allen and Unwin.

Evans, Christopher. 1973. Cults of Unreason. New York: Dell.

Festinger, Leon, H.W. Riecken, and S. Schachter. 1956. When Prophecy Fails. New York: Harper.

Flammonde, Paris. 1975. The Mystic Healers. New York: Stein and Day.

Frank, Jerome D. 1963. Persuasion and Healing. New York: Schocken.

Freud, Sigmund. 1962 (1930). Civilization and its Discontents. New York: Norton.

1964 (1927). The Future of an Illusion. Garden City, N.Y.: Doubleday.

Gardner, Martin. 1957. Fads and Fallacies in the Name of Science. New York: Dover.

Glick, Rush G., and Robert S. Newsom. 1974. Fraud Investigation. Springfield, Illinois: Thomas.

Greenberg, Joel. 1979. "Close encounters—all in the mind?" *Science News* 115:106-107.

Gurr, Ted Robert. 1970. Why Men Rebel. Princeton: Princeton University.

Hubbard, L. Ron. 1950. Dianetics, The Modern Science of Mental Health. New York: Paperback Library.

King, Francis. 1970. The Rites of Modern Occult Magic. New York: Macmillan.

Kornbluth, Jesse. 1976. "The Fuhrer over est." *New Times,* March 19:36-52.

LaBarre, Weston. 1969. They Shall Take up Serpents. New York: Schocken.

1972. The Ghost Dance. New York: Dell.

Lemert, Edwin. 1967. "Paranoia and the dynamics of exclusion." Pp. 246-264 in Edwin Lemert, *Human Deviance, Social Problems and Social Control.* Englewood Cliffs, New Jersey: Prentice-Hall.

Lévi-Strauss, Claude. 1963. "The sorcerer and his magic." Pp. 161-180 in Claude Lévi-Strauss, *Structural Anthropology.* New York: Basic Books.

Lewis, Ioan M. 1971. Ecstatic Religion. Baltimore: Penguin.

Lofland, John, and Rodney Stark. 1965. "Becoming a world-saver: a theory of conversion to a deviant perspective." *American Sociological Review* 30:862-875.

McIntosh, Christopher. 1972. Eliphas Lévi and the French Occult Revival. New York: Weiser.

Messing, Simon D. 1958. "Group therapy and social status in the Zar cult of Ethiopia." *American Anthropologist* 60:1120-1126.

Orrmont, Arthur. 1961. Love Cults and Faith Healers. New York: Ballantine.

Randi, James. 1975. The Magic of Uri Geller. New York: Ballantine.

Regardie, Israel. 1971. My Rosicrucian Adventure. St. Paul: Llewellyn.

Rieff, Philip. 1968. The Triumph of the Therapeutic. New York: Harper.

Roberts, Edward B. 1969. "Entrepreneurship and technology." Pp. 219-237 in William H. Gruber and Donald G. Marquis (eds.), *Factors in the Transfer of Technology.* Cambridge: M.I.T. Press.

Roheim, Geza. 1955. Magic and Schizophrenia. Bloomington: Indiana University.

Sargant, William. 1959. Battle for the Mind. New York: Harper and Row.

Silverman, Julian. 1967. "Shamans and acute schizophrenia." *American Anthropologist* 69:21-32.

Smelser, Neil J. 1962. Theory of Collective Behavior. New York: Free Press.

Stark, Rodney. 1965. "A sociological definition of religion." Pp. 3-17 in Charles Y. Glock and Rodney Stark, *Religion and Society in Tension.* Chicago: Rand McNally.

Stark, Rodney, and William Sims Bainbridge. 1979. "Of churches, sects, and cults: preliminary concepts for a theory of religious movements." *Journal for the Scientific Study of Religion* 18:117-131.

1980a. "Networks of faith: interpersonal bonds and recruitment to cults and sects." *American Journal of Sociology.* 85:1376-95.

1980b. "Towards a theory of religion: religious commitment." *Journal for the Scientific Study of Religion.* 19:114-28.

Wallace, Anthony F.C. 1956. "Revitalization movements." *American Anthropologist* 58:264-281.

Wallis, Roy. 1977. The Road to Total Freedom: A Sociological Analysis of Scientology. New York: Columbia University.

Zweig, Stefan. 1932. Mental Healers. New York: Viking.

3

THE PURSUIT OF INNOCENCE: NEW RELIGIOUS MOVEMENTS AND MORAL ACCOUNTABILITY

Frederick Bird

Contemporary religious movements have been analyzed from a number of perspectives. They have been viewed as expressions of a new, experimental outlook on life (Wuthnow, 1976), as aspects of a great American awakening (McLoughlin, 1978), as rescue missions for former drug users and political activists (Robbins and Anthony, 1972; Tipton, 1978), and as the manifestation of a new culture of narcissism (Lasch, 1979). The present essay examines yet another attribute characteristic of most religious movements, namely their impact on feelings of moral accountability.

Unexpectedly, we find that these movements, unlike most traditional denominational religions, tend to encourage among their adherents a reduced sense of moral accountability. While that result is achieved in a significantly different manner depending on the nature of the group, it occurs in all types of movements, and it constitutes for participants one of the appealing aspects of these new religions. When we analyze the contemporary moral milieu, we discover that its moral pluralism and relativism and its emphasis on expressive as well as institutional norms (Turner, 1975) tend on the whole to aggravate feelings of moral accountability (Bird, 1979). In that light, the emergence and growth of new religious movements seem to have occurred in part as a response to this contemporary moral dilemma. Because these movements help ease feelings of moral accountability, adherents may largely avoid moral risk and

This paper is based on data collected by a group research project at Concordia University, Montreal, funded in part by the Quebec Ministry of Education. I am grateful to the following persons who helped gather field notes, interviews, and survey data: Susan Bernstein, Scott Davidson, Bill Reimer, Darrell Leavitt, Susan Palmer, Elizabeth Sandul, Joan Perry, Hugh Shankland, Steve Paull, Bill Wheeler, Judith Strutt, Katherine McMorrow, Karina Rosenberg, and Frances Westley. I am grateful to Frances Westley for a critical reading of several drafts of this paper.

responsibility in some cases, and in others they may actively assume moral responsibility in more measured and limited terms.

Moral accountability is defined here as the *individual awareness that a person is expected to act in keeping with moral expectations*. These moral expectations may include social rules and laws, religious sanctions, routine interpersonal demands, role expectations, personal standards of excellence, and internally held notions about what significant others expect. A sense of moral accountability ordinarily involves an awareness of the relationship or discrepancy between a person's actual activities and these moral expectations, between action and intention, between ego and ego ideal (Bird, 1977). This sense of moral accountability may be accompanied by feelings of personal satisfaction or dissatisfaction, of justification or guilt. But moral accountability is not the same thing as moral responsibility, for the latter involves not merely an awareness but also the personal avowing of obligations in relation to oneself and others and the acknowledging of one's answerability for their realization. The impact of participation in religious movements on moral responsibility is a separate and more complex issue outside the scope of this paper.[1]

Our analysis focuses on new religious movements which have proliferated in North America since the late 1960s, classified in three distinct groups according to the relationship of followers to masters or the relationship of the religious seekers to the sacred power they revere. In these groups adherents typically become either (a) *devotees* of a sacred lord or lordly truth, (b) *disciples* of a revered and holy discipline, (c) or *apprentices* skilled at unlocking the mysteries of a sacred, inner power. In the *devotee* pattern, members ultimately surrender themselves to a holy master or ultimate reality to whom they attribute superhuman powers and consciousness. This pattern occurs in congregational groups such as Catholic and Protestant Charismatics, the Divine Light Mission, the Nichirin Shoshu Academy, the followers of Sri Chinmoy and the International Society for Krishna Consciousness. *Disciples* progressively seek to master spiritual and/or physical disciplines in order to achieve a state of enlightenment and self-harmony, often following the example of a revered teacher. This pattern is found in the Integral Yoga Institute, Dharmadatu groups, Zen centers, and Tai Chi Ch'uan. In *apprenticeship* groups (see Westley, 1978b), participants seek to master particular psychic, shamanic and therapeutic skills in order to tap and realize sacred powers within themselves. This pattern occurs

[1]Moral responsibility involves choice and decision, not merely awareness. To gauge the actual influence of new religious movements on moral responsibility would require careful case studies of a fairly broad sample of adherents and non-adherents. It is also worth noting that for some persons the reduction of feelings of moral accountability not only frees them from feelings of moral inadequacy but also seems to encourage a more lively sense of responsibility. But the opposite pattern also occurs.

in groups like Psychosynthesis, Silva Mind Control, EST, Arica, Transcendental Meditation and Scientology.[2]

Devotees, disciples and apprentices seek to realize similar feelings of reduced moral accountability, but in strikingly different ways, according to (a) the *relationship of participants to sacred power,* (b) the group's *form of authority,* and (c) the *moral model* the group holds. Sacred power is a revered source of personal energy that must be protected from everyday routines and interactions which can profane and dissipate its potency. The felt location of this power is related to the authority structure of the group, and both dimensions have implications for its moral model, the moral prescriptions to which members must adhere. Because participants experience these dimensions most fully during the initiation process, our analysis draws heavily, but not exclusively, on data from initiation rituals for illustrative purposes. We first identify the different means used in each type of group, then discuss their common result, the reduction of moral accountability. In conclusion, we suggest that a number of features of contemporary society combine to exacerbate a sense of moral accountability without increasing the possibility of control, and that these groups, in their various ways, offer a resolution, albeit a temporary one, to this dilemma.

DEVOTEE GROUPS

1. *Relation to Sacred Power.* Initiates into devotee groups revere what they consider to be an ultimate source of self-power and truth, whether identified as

[2]This typology corresponds in part to that developed by Anthony and Robbins (Anthony, et. al., 1978). There is a correlation between what Anthony and Robbins identify as one step, technical, monistic groups, what I have identified as apprenticeship groups and what Westley has identified as Cult of Man groups (Westley, 1978a). There is also a correlation between what Anthony and Robbins refer to as two step, technical, monistic groups and what I have identified as discipleship groups. My typology differs from Anthony and Robbins in several other respects. (a) I have argued that a number of groups arising out of Christian, Buddhist, and Hindu traditions all contain belief, ritual and authority patterns that approximate what I have referred to as devotee type groups. All revere a sacred, transcendent, omnipresent Other, develop congregations, and uphold explicit moral expectations. Although elsewhere I have argued that all new religious and para-religious movements can be fittingly described as being most like inner-worldly mystical movements (Bird and Reimer, 1976), all these devotee groups tend to exhibit marked sectarian and ascetic characteristics. (b) I disagree in part with Anthony and Robbins about the extent to which a number of groups adhere to monistic or dualistic moral philosophies. I remain uneasy with their identification of all eastern religions as monistic, not only because of the ontological and ethical dualisms which seem to be inter-related with Hindu Vedantism (see Weber 1961, section on the Ethics of the Gita), but also because the significant difference between religions arising out of Buddhist, Muslim, Hindu and Taoist traditions are blurred by this use of the term ''eastern.'' A number of the groups which they identify as being monistic, I would argue can be more accurately and fruitfully analyzed either (1) as being gnostic and hence dualistic (groups like Gurdjieff or Transcendental Meditation or perhaps even Psychosynthesis) because of their significant devaluation of everyday routines in relation to inner knowledge or (2) as being sectarian and to a degree dualistic (groups like NSA) because of their strong in-group feelings, the identification of their movements with a world-saving mission and their active proselytizing.

God, Krishna, or the Buddhist Truth of the Lotus Sutra. This sacred power is an objectively existing, self-transcending and omnipresent reality. No special qualifications except faith are needed to enter into relationships with it, although perceptions and loyalties do need to be reoriented to become more accessible to its influence. For example, initiation rites in devotee groups assume the form of an induction into a congregation whose collective rituals serve as an indispensable means or occasion for making sacred reality present and accessible. This process begins with a period of intense interaction with other group members, whether in the form of the weekend sessions held by the Unification Church or the more leisurely Seminars of the Spirit held by the Catholic Charismatics. Through this interaction and participation in group activities, the potential initiate becomes aware of the nature of the ultimate reality as defined by the group and of the demands which that reality places upon him or her as an individual. These demands include both mundane folkways (such as the tacit rejection of alcohol or encouragement to vegetarianism among the Charismatics or Sri Chinmoy) and restrictive norms which govern every aspect of life (such as those found in the Unification Church or Hare Krishna). Often, however, it seems to the initiates that they are not so much rationally selecting a way of life but responding spontaneously and emotionally to an intense experience of being enfolded in a loving and accepting communal embrace to which, at last, they yield. The period of interaction is one of mutual opening of the group to the individual and of the individual to the group. The actual moment of initiation, the act of commitment itself, is often one of intense emotional experience. For the new Charismatic, the Baptism of the Spirit is often associated with the first experience of glossolalia, with spontaneous tears and sometimes with trance-like behaviour. The Divine Light initiate experiences a moment of intense and mystical insight also often accompanied by trance. The experience is typically described by initiates themselves as one of rebirth and renewal (cf. Gerlach and Hine, 1970).

   2. *Authority Structure.* In devotee groups the ultimate authority is a revered, self-transcending Other. Initiates surrender to this sacred power both objectively, by submitting in their inductions to the authority and direction of the group, and subjectively in trance-like states, by identifying their real self with this sacred Other. For example, Charismatics seek to be more responsive to the daily direction of the Holy Spirit and also to surrender to its influence while experiencing glossolalia. Similarly, Nichirin members devote themselves to following the guidance of the Lotus Sutra and pledge themselves to adhere to the direction of the president of this international movement. They seek to become one with the truth and being of this sutra by chanting its Japanese name. In all these devotee groups, initiates submit to relatively autocratic sacred authorities who are believed to exercise a considerable degree

of day to day guidance over their lives, both through explicit group directions and through occasional personal inspirations.

In many of these groups, initiates' relation to sacred power and its historical representatives is thought to be like the relation of children to a sovereign but benevolent parent, who on some occasions ironically seems to appear like a playful and innocent child. For example, Sri Chinmoy followers describe themselves as children and their master and his consort as Father and Mother. Yet when they meditate in his presence, he often appears as a speechless child who needs help to be fed. Divine Light initiates often refer to Guru Maharaj Ji as an alternative and more benign parent, but they also take delight in his childish antics. Likewise, Krishna followers describe Krishna as a ruling Lord and their leader Swami Bhativedanta as a Father, yet they too delight in the legend about Krishna as a playful boy in somewhat different forms. Charismatics view themselves as being freshly born children of the Father, who is also believed to be a lively, spontaneous, joyful and innocent Spirit. Typically, it is the presence of these holy beings which is revered—by honoring or worshipping their names or pictures in chants, songs or silence—rather than their philosophies, doctrines or prophetic messages.

3. *Moral Model.* Devotee groups usually uphold fairly explicit sets of moral prescriptions, which vary in content from group to group. These groups place an emphasis on performance, including both positive adherence to prescriptive standards and the forswearing of proscribed practices and loyalties. To some degree these groups represent a reassertion of traditional, non-utilitarian ascetic standards, but what is important from a comparative perspective is that devotees are not free to select at will among these performance norms. In most of these groups, members also are obligated to undertake some form of ministry, either by actively proselytizing (Hare Krishna and Nichirin) or by taking responsibility for special group activities (Charismatic or Sri Chinmoy groups).

APPRENTICESHIP GROUPS

1. *Relation to Sacred Power.* Adherents of apprenticeship groups assume that there are revered, objectively existing sources of energy for greater self power which are immanent within each individual. For example, Silva Mind Control trainees seek to tap inner powers to become psychics; TM meditators seek to make contact with the hidden, internal sources of creative intelligence; and students of Psychosynthesis seek to activate the inner self which is a source of cosmic energies. In their initiation rituals, designed to gain access to these fields of energy, initiates learn a series of techniques and exercises and direct their psychic energies while practicing these techniques away from external,

distracting influences and from preexisting, false notions of themselves. To learn these practices, initiates pass through an initiatory ordeal, during which there is some restriction on their freedom of motion. The passage may be relatively strenuous in groups like Arica or EST or so simple and easy, as in Transcendental Meditation, that initiates have almost no sense of an ordeal at all. A certificate is ordinarily received at the completion of the ordeal.

In all these apprenticeship groups the immanent source of sacred power is identified with an internal, higher self, differentiated from the ego and personality. Initiates are instructed that their real self, which is to be protected from profane, careless exposure, is to be identified not with their relative roles, changing configurations of their personalities, or even transient unconscious associations, but with an unchanging, higher, transcendent self or ego. This transcendent ego is not conceived as the locus of moral sentiment, such as the superego or Durkheim's moral self. Rather, it has variously been conceived as the source of individual uniqueness, as an impersonal dimension of personhood, as the source (but not the processes) of consciousness, as the observing subject, and as a more abiding ground of selfhood than the transient impressions of ordinarily self-consciousness. Students of Gurdjieff are counseled, for example, that their real selves are not their anxious, troubled, and transient egos but their transcendent, largely undiscovered selves. TM initiates are told that their real selves exist not in the pitter-patter of their daily thoughts but in the depths of their consciousness. Followers of Psychosynthesis are informed that their real, essential selves are their transcendent egos. All these apprenticeship groups identify the real self neither with cluttered cognitive processes nor with volitional activities, but with a subjective, uncluttered, enlightened awareness.

2. *Authority Structure.* The leaders of these apprenticeship groups are all viewed as enlightened masters. José Silva (Silva Mind Control), Maharishi Mahesh Yogi (Transcendental Meditation), Oscar Ichazo (Arica), Robert Assigioli (Psychosynthesis), Werner Erhart (EST), and Ron Hubbard (Scientology) have acted relatively autocratically in establishing these various groups and in claiming validity, both absolute and pragmatic, for their movements. They all serve as the supreme legislators and executives of their respective movements, founded on their own inspired but semi-scientific discoveries, and they all claim a considerable degree of obedience from their instructors. But their ordinary adherents are much less obedient, for they simply purchase knowledge of the techniques they receive through the initiatory ordeal. After that purchase, adherents themselves become the arbiters of how they utilize this newly acquired knowledge and skill. To be sure, during the ordeal itself, the group often exercises nearly complete authority over initiates by severely limiting their freedom of movement. Complaints about this autocratic authority, voiced in particular with regard to EST and Arica, contrast sharply with the

discretion adherents experience once this initiation process has been completed. Having completed the ordeal, initiates are no longer answerable to these groups or to their leaders.[3]

3. *Moral Model*. Apprenticeship groups uphold moral models which place highest priority on two inter-related activities: (a) developing the personal power and effectiveness of each individual, and (b) protecting the higher, inner self from contaminating, confusing and threatening environmental influences. Apprentices are instructed, in the language of EST, to see themselves as "cause in matter," or in other words, to develop greater control over their personal and environmental interactions. They are variously instructed to act from their own center rather than in response or allegiance to external demands. This greater self-control is believed to be achieved by practicing the special techniques of these groups and by placing greater confidence in the inner perfection of the self. The purpose of meditation is to block out external, stressful, confusing impressions (TM and Silva Mind Control) and to detach self-identity from ego defenses or from nostalgia for and regrets about the past (EST and Arica). The message is that the real self is a transpersonal, transcendent ego which is essentially good and which can act effectively and creatively if not distracted. Adherents of apprenticeship groups are counseled to assume a non-judgmental attitude toward their performances and actions. What matters is not how well one performs in relation to some arbitrary standard but that each person acts from his own center. As a result, apprenticeship groups foster two additional moral attitudes: (a) a concern to achieve a minimal degree of self-awareness capable of distinguishing the real, higher transpersonal selves from the outer and transitory self-impressions, and (b) a non-judgmental tolerance for the activities of others.

DISCIPLESHIP GROUPS

1. *Relation to Sacred Power*. Adherents of discipleship groups have little notion of an objectively existing field of energy or power, whether self-transcending or immanent. Their aim is not to gain access to additional sources of energy but to conserve the tremendous dissipation of existing human energy. Their goal is not to transmit energy from without through an induction, or from within through an ordeal, but to discipline one's whole life for the purposes of eventually gaining enlightenment and of immediately enjoying greater physical and mental well-being. Initiates seek to learn and to master various mental and physical exercises. Such learning and mastery take much time and effort. Hence, in almost all discipleship movements there are multiple initiation rites.

[3] In apprenticeship groups, those who become instructors often assume a closer, more tutelary relation with the leaders. As teachers, they allow the group to offer them more explicit directions.

The initial introductory rites are usually informal and frequently involve nothing more than the impersonal permission to become a student of the discipline. Subsequent initiatory rites are more formalized. Initiation rites at the higher ranks ordinarily take the form of ordination rites, for which particular adherents qualify in part by their own mastery of the discipline.

Most yoga students, for example, simply register for courses initially and are only subsequently invited to participate in more demanding and exacting exercises and in regular, comparatively taxing meditation sessions. Similarly, Tai Chi adherents simply enroll in classes at the beginning but over time seek to achieve more perfect mastery over the physical movements of this discipline and to attune their minds more closely to the Taoist philosophy as exemplified by their teacher-leaders. In all these discipleship groups, initiates seek over time to gain greater self-power largely by gaining greater control and discipline over their physical, mental and emotional energies. They aim to identify their real self neither with a Transcendent Being nor with a higher, inner, transpersonal self; the idea of an inner, real self is in fact foreign to groups like Dharmadatu and Zen Centers, which arose out of Buddhist traditions. Rather they seek to discover their real self in a harmonized, whole, one-pointed state of mindbody. Hence the physical and mental disciplines are interrelated in these groups.

2. *Authority Structures*. The masters of these various disciplines are neither human avatars like Sri Chinmoy or Guru Maharaj Ji nor revered founders/discoverers like José Silva or Maharishi Mahesh Yogi. They are at once merely contemporary transmitters passing on to their followers centuries-old disciplines and philosophies, exemplary prophets who through their own training and dedication have mastered these disciplines, and masters who demand a measure of allegiance from their disciples. The relation of Swami Satchidanda (Integral Yoga Institute), or Swami Vishnudevanda (Sivananda Yoga), or Master Lee (Tai Chi), or Philip Kapleau (Zen) or Choygam Trumpa Rimpoche (Dharmadatu) to their disciples can all be similarly described. Unlike the masters of some devotee groups, they assume no protective concern for their followers. But the followers, as they continue to enroll in more advanced classes and practice their exercises and meditation, allow the group to assume a greater measure of direction over their lives.

3. *Moral Model*. The moral models which these discipleship groups advocate assign priority to three inter-related values: (a) the cultivation of a detached yet compassionate inner disposition as a virtue, (b) the attempt to establish personal harmony, and (c) the effort to realize these aims through self-discipline. This inner disposition is seen as being at once detached—morally indifferent to the vicissitudes of everyday historical existence—and compassionate—accepting the world as it is without rancor. These groups do not insist

on maintaining particular norms with regard to personal behavior, nor do they encourage what has traditionally been called character development. Rather, this inner disposition is pursued as an intrinsically valued end which can only be fully realized by practicing a discipline which modifies the conscious and pre-conscious habits of thought. Achieving an overall harmony within oneself as an embodied, feeling, conscious, and willing being is both the pre-condition and the primary expression of this valued inner disposition. This state of personal harmony is not infrequently described as a non-aggressive, non-assertive condition. Typically, disciples seek to achieve this harmonious state through both physical and mental exercises which encourage even-mindedness and balance. Students of these disciplines are encouraged to exemplify in their daily routines the inner peace realized through their meditation and exercises.

These discipleship groups counsel their students that these virtues of inner peace and personal harmony can only be attained by regular practice and by seeking the criticism and guidance of more skilled practitioners. Self-discipline itself is in various ways upheld as a pre-eminent moral value, but it ordinarily is conceived merely as a prudential counsel of excellence, not an obligatory requirement. If students do not attain higher levels of skill and consciousness, they are not reprimanded or expelled. These increasingly exacting standards of excellence serve as models for greater aspiration. Hence these standards can be utilized to evaluate in a non-judgmental fashion the spiritual practices of disciples at various levels of accomplishment.

HOW THESE GROUPS FOSTER REDUCED
FEELINGS OF MORAL ACCOUNTABILITY

By means of their own particular constellation of ideas about sacred power, patterns of authority and models of morality, these three types of groups foster among their adherents comparable, reduced feelings of moral accountability. In contrasting ways, these groups realize this condition (a) by relativizing or diminishing the extent to which participants feel *morally answerable to others*, (b) by decreasing adherents' own feeling of *self-accountability*, and (c) by supporting moral models which reduce the *sense of difference between actual behavior and moral expectations*.

Many of these groups openly announce their interest in helping participants to reduce their feelings of moral accountability and to enhance their sense of innocence. Scientologists, for example, seek to attain a state of mind called CLEAR; TM meditators seek to unstress; Divine Light premies seek to be one with the saving yet worldly innocence of their master; Tai Chi participants seek to realize a peaceful equanimity beyond good and evil, assertion and defense; Zen initiates seek to realize emptiness; and Krishna devotees seek to think only of Krishna. In none of these groups are there rites for directly confronting the destructive or morally ambiguous dimension of self or even the self-perceived discrepancies between intention and action through confession, atonement, or free associations.

Initiates into all these various groups experience a decreased degree of answerability to others outside their groups as they defer to the comparatively autocratic authority patterns of these groups. By acknowledging these authorities, they gain thereby a kind of license, a derived sense of personal authority, which authorizes them to ignore or to count as of only relative importance the claims made by various other secular authorities. It is interesting to notice the largely unexamined ways in which deference to these charismatic and often autocratic authorities seems ironically to enhance initiates' own sense of personal discretion. In pluralistic society where persons are often confronted with multiple, conflicting authority claims in relation to work, life style, beliefs and personal relations, acquiring a license that encourages and allows persons to screen out some of these claims may indeed indirectly enhance their sense of personal autonomy. This enhancement may occur even when gaining such a license means submitting to a given, comparably autocratic authority.

In fact, the strength of this personal license seems in part to be a product of the power of particular authority relations from which it is derived. In other respects, however, these contemporary, non-traditional religious movements reduce feelings of moral accountability in somewhat different ways.

1. *Devotee Groups.* Initiates into devotee groups often allow these associations to become their dominant reference group. Other moral expectations, related to worldly success in career or personal relationships, are relativized in relation to the demands and expectations of these groups. These expectations seem to fit together in a coherent whole that is manageable, even if somewhat demanding. While accountability to others is reduced by adopting a new, supportive reference group, self-accountability also is diminished as adherents identify their real selves with their sacred alter egos. These various sacred Others are believed to look after the welfare of their devotees along with and by means of these congregations of fellow devotees. Devotees variously believe that if they chant before a Gohonza, recite the name of Krishna, meditate on the picture of the face of Sri Chinmoy, or pray for the guidance of the Holy Spirit, they will be able to act decisively without worry and self-doubt in ambiguous situations. They feel that some of the worry and responsibility for how to act is borne by these sacred beings (Westley, 1977). Although these groups maintain certain moral models, these are primarily related to activities of the group. Devotees' own sense of moral ambiguity is further lessened because in none of these groups are the self-transcending sacred Powers with which they identify envisioned as judges or rulers like Biblical and Qur'anic deities. Devotees say

that they feel good about themselves because these Masters do not require from them any accounting of past and present plans and activities.

(A Divine Light Premie) But one thing I experienced, or don't experience any more, when I get into these things is that I don't experience guilt. Guru Maharaj Ji loves me so much ... he gives to me every day ... .I don't feel any stress ... just feel good. Guru Maharaj Ji doesn't leave me alone ... .we are all Guru Maharaj Ji's children ... sometimes I sit for a long time (meditating) and nothing happens ... but the minute we let go, the love is there .... there is no past (Anthony, et al., 1977:868, 872).

(Description of Sri Chinmoy meditation) You don't want to go anywhere here, not even out of this blue and white room. You just want to sit in Guruji's lap of abstractions and curly smiles and sleepy eyes and drift off to perfection rest.

As a consequence of this relationship of personal devotion, participants in these movements tend to view themselves, they say, in less judgmental terms. It is not that feelings of guilt and moral dissatisfaction have been overcome or redressed but rather that there are fewer occasions for these feelings to arise at all.

2. *Apprenticeship Groups.* Adherents of apprenticeship groups reduce their feelings of accountability to others in two ways. First, they are instructed that they are the arbiters of their own destiny and of how to utilize the techniques and processes learned in these groups. Second, they are counseled to relativize or discount other standards of achievement in comparison to their own sense of accomplishment with the techniques acquired in their initiatory ordeal. As Don Juan tells his apprentice, Carlos Castaneda, it is not what others think that matters, since they are often blinded by confusion and superficial appearance, thereby lacking true vision and knowledge. Apprentices reduce their feelings of self-accountability by identifying their real selves with an amoral, transpersonal, ahistorical awareness. Such a sense of self is associated not with feelings of willful accountability but rather with a mindful awareness, innocent of any notions of judgment and evaluation. Feelings of moral ambiguity are lessened in a like manner by identifying the inner, higher self as essentially good and the other aspects of self as transitory and morally indifferent.

These modes of reducing feelings of moral accountability can be illustrated by the particularly restricted meaning which a group like EST attaches to the notion of responsibility, an idea frequently used with an amoral meaning.

Responsibility starts with the willingness to acknowledge that you are cause in matter ... you are the source of what you are, what you do, and what you have .... Responsibility is not fault, blame, shame, or guilt. All these include judgments and evaluations of good and bad, right and wrong, or better and worse ... they are all beyond a simple acknowledgement that you are cause in your own experience (Stone, 1978:67).

Responsibility is here defined in a way that excludes accountability to moral standards, the expectations of others, or one's own principles. Further, there is an implicit identification of intention with action which excludes guilt; people experience what they cause themselves to experience, and they realize what they choose to realize.

3. *Discipleship Groups.* In discipleship groups adherents diminish and relativize their feelings of accountability to others by assigning personal priority both to their allegiance to their masters and disciplines and to their personal goal of realizing a more harmonious, detached state of mind. Other secular goals and expectations are not infrequently made secondary to the pursuit of this inner sense of balance and equanimity. For example, the overly assertive pursuit of success in career has been characterized by a Tai Chi master as an example of an abrasive, aggressive spirit (Wong, 1976).

Interestingly, discipleship groups continue to stress the importance of self-accountability. Their valorization of self-discipline is an expression of this concern. Even the maxim that practitioners of these disciplines should carry into their everyday activities the inner peace which they realize in their meditation demands that these students act with a degree of moral self-reflection. However, feelings of self-accountability are modified by two decisive factors both of which result in reduced feelings of moral ambiguity. First, rather than being evaluated in relation to judgmental standards of obligation, disciples' accomplishments are to be evaluated by themselves in relation to permissive standards of excellence and aspiration. Such standards tend to ease and soften feelings of accountability. Adherents are counseled that students of these disciplines ordinarily are able to arrive at somewhat different levels of accomplishment. In addition, discipleship groups stress that while it is necessary to perform meditations and exercises in accord with a pattern of discipline, the highest virtue is represented not by a form of behavior but by an inner disposition of detached compassion. In relation to this virtue it is inappropriate to judge one's own efforts too severely. Such attitudes represent confusing attachment to some external standards of success. What really matters is that disciples seek to realize this inner balance.

THE CONTEMPORARY APPEAL OF THESE GROUPS: THE MODERN DILEMMA OF MORAL ACCOUNTABILITY

These varied new religious and para-religious movements all foster among their participants reduced feelings of moral accountability or put another way, enhanced feelings of innocence. In this respect, these groups differ from traditional Christian and Jewish denominations which uphold sacred authority patterns and moral models that heighten or at least reinforce feelings of moral accountability. Such feelings are in fact confirmed by rites for confession and atonement which provide means by which adherents may compensate for or overcome these feelings. These movements also differ from psychoanalytic therapy in which clients are called upon to acknowledge, avow and assume more insightful responsibility for their own lives (Fingarette, 1965; 1969). It is therefore appropriate to ask why this wide variety of new religious and para-religious movements, all of which seem to foster among their adherents reduced feelings of moral accountability, have arisen and flourished in contemporary society.

In approaching this issue, it is well to recognize that the interest in reducing feelings of moral accountability is not confined to new religious movements. There are a number of other expressions of this contemporary pursuit of innocence. For example, several observers have noted the increasing tendency to deal with moral dilemmas in terms of technical practicality or personal preference rather than in relation to norms about right behavior or standards of virtue. From a different perspective, Reich (1970) argues that a revolution in consciousness has been occurring, especially among the younger generations, who place less emphasis on external standards of performance and seek instead to act with a natural spontaneity. Others identify these shifts in attitude, especially among the younger generations, with a form of nostalgia for pre-oedipal childhood, when persons were cared for by benevolent authorities, experienced little guilt in relation to emotional alterations, and felt no need to spell out or to acknowledge their own feelings of destructiveness and failure. And the pursuit of innocence, however evaluated, seems also to be evident among many Christian denominations, in which the rituals either for corporate or for personal confession have lost their prominence (cf. Reich, 1970; May, 1972; Menninger, 1973; Berger, et. al., 1974; Rieff, 1970; Turner, 1975).

However widespread, this pursuit of innocence does not arise by accident. The interest in new religious groups or therapies in which persons can experience reduced feelings of moral accountability is rather a response to what I shall term the *modern dilemma of moral accountability*.[4] The characteristic feature of this dilemma is that diffuse feelings of moral accountability have been aggravated, somewhat ironically, by a cultural situation in which multiple, relativistic and comparatively permissive moral expectations have supplanted a fairly unified system of more strict moral standards.

Traditionally, persons often identified what they should do by following rules associated with various institutions—state, religion, kin group, or occupational group. These rules were authoritatively established by customs or

---

[4]The moral dilemma examined here is different from, though related to, what Bell (1976) and Habermas (1975) have described as the legitimation crisis experienced by industrial capitalism in mass consumer societies governed by a welfare state.

official enactment and were defended by rational discourse of a legal or philosophical character. Persons often formally acknowledged the authority of these rules by participating in initiatory rites of puberty and induction marking entrance into these institutions. However, as a result of complex forces set in motion by industrialization, democratization, and secularization, traditional moral rules have lost much of their authority. They have been supplemented by a widely acknowledged, yet diffuse, utilitarian ethic. In contemporary society persons move in and out of multiple institutions, all with various explicit and implicit norms, some traditional and many largely utilitarian. Hence, for many persons a contextual, often positivistic "ethic of the fitting" serves as an appropriate moral guide. However, this ethic of the fitting has been supplemented by what might be called a psychological "ethic of self-realization," in which moral good is identified not in relation to institutional expectations but in relation to feelings of personal well-being. To the question, "what should I do?" the reply is given "One should be true to one's own feelings."

This historical shift in the kinds of standards used for making moral choices has had some unexpectedly ambiguous and largely unexamined consequences for the sense of moral accountability. The increasing relativity of moral standards has, no doubt, eased some of the sense of moral accountability. To the extent that they participate in various institutions, though, persons feel a partial obligation both to abide by the normative expectations of these institutions and to pay attention, however imperfectly, to their own feelings. Moreover, many persons retain a sense of accountability to parents and to their values long after they have formally left home and established their own standards and ideals. The personal sense of moral accountability thus is aggravated by the fact that it is often difficult to make sense of or to achieve a manageable balance among various external and internal moral expectations. Furthermore, feelings of moral accountability, are increased as people feel they are responsible for the condition of their own health and personal well-being, as well as for how they act in relation to particular norms. The personal sense of failing, confusion or disapproval, therefore, cannot be blamed on institutional norms or role expectations. As a result, persons experience moral unease not only by occasionally violating some traditional and absolutist moral standards which they only partially honor but also by violating their own intentions or personal promises, by trespassing on the feelings of their friends or associates, by failing to live up to their expected performance in various roles or institutions, and by failing to make into a coherent whole the various, often disordered aspects of their lives.

Several different strategies may be adopted in relation to these diffuse yet pervasive feelings of increased moral accountability. A traditional ethic of an established religion or a contemporary ideology may be embraced, thus reducing the personal sense of accountability but also reducing the range of personal choices. An intense and long tutelary apprenticeship with a confessor/ analyst may be undertaken in order to fully acknowledge one's own account- ability with stoic courage-to-be. Or a decrease in the sense of moral account- ability may be sought by attempting to augment the sense of innocence in a variety of ways. One of the appeals of new religious movements is that they provide one such means for realizing a somewhat reduced sense of moral accountability. As such, new religious movements serve an unannounced, and frequently unrecognized, therapeutic function that is still widely sought after. They help to ease feelings of moral accountability in decisively different ways, briefly sketched above, which leave adherents with varying degrees of their own sense of discretion, autonomy and responsibility. In their variety, these movements may therefore be viewed both as *expressions of* the contemporary moral milieu, with its relativisms and focus on personal, private moral codes, and as organized *responses to* feelings of moral confusion occasioned by this milieu.

REFERENCES

Anthony, Dick, Thomas Curtis, Madeline Doucas, and Thomas Robbins. 1977. "Patients and pilgrims." *American Behavioral Scientist* 20, 6: 861-886.

Anthony, Dick, Thomas Robbins, and James Richardson. 1978. "Theory and research on today's 'new religions.' " *Sociological Analysis* 39: 95-122.

Bell, Daniel. 1976. The Cultural Contradictions of Capitalism. New York: Basic Books.

Berger, Brigitte, Peter Berger, and Hansfried Kellner. 1974. The Homeless Mind: Modernization and Consciousness. New York: Random House.

Bird, Frederick, and William Reimer. 1976. "A sociological analysis of new religious and para-religious movements." In *Canadian Religion*. Crusdale: MacMillan Press.

Bird, Frederick. 1977. "False consciousness as a moral problem." Presented to the Annual Meeting of the Society for the Scientific Study of Religion, Chicago.

1979. "Paradigms and parameters in the comparative study of religious and ideo- logical ethics." Canadian Society for the Study of Religion.

Fingarette, Herbert. 1965. The Self in Transformation. New York: Harper.

1969. Self-Deception. London: Routledge and Kegan Paul.

Gerlach, Luther, and Virginia Hine. 1970. People, Power and Change. Indianapo- lis: Bobbs-Merrill.

Habermas, Jurgen. 1975. Legitimation Crisis. Tr. Thomas McCarthy. Boston: Beacon.

Lasch, Christopher. 1979. The Culture of Narcissism. New York: Norton.

May, Rollo. 1972. Power and Innocence. New York: Norton.

McLoughlin, William G. 1978. Revivals, Awakenings, and Reform. Chicago: University of Chicago.

Menninger, Karl. 1973. Whatever Became of Sin? New York: Bantam.

Reich, Charles. 1970. The Greening of America. New York: Random House.

Rieff, Philip. 1970. The Triumph of the Therapeutic. New York: Random House.

Robbins, Thomas, and Dick Anthony. 1972. "Getting straight with Meher Baba." Journal for the Scientific Study of Religion 8: 308-13.

Stone, Donald. 1978. "The human potential movement." Society 15 (4): 66-68.

Tipton, Steve. 1978. Getting Saved from the Sixties. Unpublished PhD. Dissertation. Harvard University.

Turner, Ralph. 1975. "The real self; from institution to impulse." American Journal of Sociology 81: 989-1016.

Weber, Max. 1961. The Religion of India. Tr. H.H. Gerth. New York: Free Press.

Westley, Frances. 1977. "Searching for surrender." American Behavioral Scientist.

1978a. "The cult of man: Durkheimian predictions and new religious movements." Sociological Analysis 39: 135-45.

1978b. The Complex Forms of the Religious Life: A Durkheimian View of the New Religious Movements. Unpublished PhD. Dissertation. McGill University.

Wong, Maria. 1976. The Teaching of Master Lee. Unpublished Master's Thesis. Concordia University.

Wuthnow, Robert. 1976. The Consciousness Reformation. Berkeley: University of California.

4

THE MOONIES AND THE ANTI-CULTISTS: MOVEMENT AND COUNTERMOVEMENT IN CONFLICT

Anson D. Shupe, Jr., David G. Bromley

The 1970s have witnessed a broadly based resurgence of religious interest and activity. While a number of mainline denominations have been losing members, fundamentalist Christian groups and a coterie of "new" religions and quasi-religions—such as the Children of God, Hare Krishna, Transcendental Meditation, Scientology, and the Unification Church—have experienced rapid growth. Although an expanding corpus of research on many of these "new" religions has recently appeared (e.g., Needleman and Baker, 1978; Glock and Bellah, 1976; Richardson, 1978; Danner, 1976; Zaretsky and Leone, 1974; Wallis, 1977), there has been considerably less research on the "anti-cult" movement (hereafter the ACM) which has emerged in response to these groups (for the major exceptions to this trend see Shupe and Bromley, 1980a, Bromley and Shupe, 1979a; Lofland, 1977: Epilogue; Enroth, 1977).

Despite the fact that the ACM is a relatively small, loose national coalition of local groups, it has had a substantial impact on the development of many "new" religions. While the ACM has gained a great deal of visibility from its most sensational (although relatively infrequently employed) tactic, coercive deprogramming, there has been virtually no examination of the ACM's emergence, structure and operation from a social movements perspective. In this paper we shall examine how the characteristics of certain of these "new" religious movements—in particular the Unification Church (or, more correctly, the Unificationist Movement, hereafter the UM), which was the primary nemesis of the ACM—led to its formation as a counter-movement. This analysis of the ACM as a counter-movement will emphasize its institutional

This paper is the product of a joint effort. The order of authorship is random and does not imply any difference in the importance of contributions.

sources and composition and how the movement's strategies and tactics flowed from both the UM's style of resource mobilization[1] and the specific interests of those institutions which spear-headed the ACM.[2] We have selected the UM as an illustrative example because of our own familiarity with it, because after 1975 ACM leaders agreed to focus their oppositional activities on the UM as the best known of the "cults" with the hope that victories against it would serve as precedents for attacking other groups, and finally, because the UM was archetypical of the characteristics the ACM most virulently condemned.

CHARACTERISTICS OF WORLD-TRANSFORMING MOVEMENTS

Not all of the "new" religions and quasi-religious groups that emerged (or re-emerged) in the United States in the late 1960s and early 1970s have been the objects of social repression to the same extent. Movements such as the Hare Krishna, the Children of God, and the UM have experienced the greatest negative reaction. These movements have sought to initiate *sweeping, structural change* of the society in which they were located. By contrast, other movements of this period, such as Transcendental Meditation, EST (Erhard Seminar Training), Meher Baba and Scientology, have engendered considerably less controversy because they promote *limited, individual change* and indeed, have functioned in many respects to adapt their members to society as it is (see Robbins *et al.,* 1978; Anthony and Robbins, 1974; Wallis, 1977). The former type of movement, which we shall refer to here as "world-transforming," is our central concern since the ACM was formed largely in response to the current wave of such movements.

We cannot discuss in detail here the nature of world-transforming movements. However, it is important to identify four sources of conflict that typically have emerged as world-transforming movements (in general), and the UM (in particular), attempt to mobilize resources to pursue their goals: (1) *ideology* (2) *organizational style,* (3) *economic resources* and (4) *recruitment and socialization practices.* As we shall show, it was precisely these issues which stimulated the formation of the ACM and around which the conflict between the UM and ACM revolved.

[1] The "resource mobilization" perspective, as developed in a growing literature, emphasizes both societal support and constraint of social movements, stressing such factors as the variety of resources which movements must mobilize, the linkage of a given movement to other groups and institutions, the dependence of movements on external support for success, and the tactics used by authorities (and other) to control or incorporate movements (cf. McCarthy and Zald, 1973, 1974, 1977; Gamson, 1975; Zald and Ash, 1973; Zald and Berger, 1978).

[2] Readers are referred to separate publications that provide specific information on fieldwork and analysis, as well as more detailed descriptions of the topics considered here (Shupe and Bromley 1980a, 1980b, Bromley and Shupe, 1979a, 1979b, 1979c; Shupe, *et. al.,* 1977a).

World-transforming movements inevitably provoke *ideological conflict.* If sweeping social change is to be justified, the movement must offer some new, unique solution to a human problem or dilemma. Since most societies have already been forced to confront these sorts of issues and have institutionalized definitions of and solutions for them, world-transforming movements challenge important assumptions underpinning the social order. In the case of the UM the challenge was primarily religious, although the implications of its theology were, in reality, considerably more pervasive. According to UM scripture, all previous religions provided only partial insight into God's purpose for mankind. For example, Moon's reformulation of Biblical history directly challenged orthodox Christian theology by asserting that Jesus had failed to accomplish his divinely commissioned task of establishing God's heavenly kingdom on earth: uniting humanity and marrying to form the first "Perfect Family." Indeed, although Moon acknowledged Jesus to be a Son of God, he was merely one in a historical series of individuals who had sought, but failed, to restore man to God. Christ thus became a role (rather than a unique personage) to which Moon himself now aspired. These and other UM claims essentially reduced other religions to a status inferior to Moon's UM which alone possessed the unique *gnosis* necessary for restoring man to God. This naturally led leaders of established churches to charge Moon with heresy, false messiahship, and counterfeit theology.

World-transforming movements by definition are *pan-institutional* in their orientation in that they usually resist the confinement of their activities to any one institutional sphere. Existing social arrangements and institutional boundaries inevitably are viewed as arbitrary; indeed world-transformation implies a reordering of social priorities and institutional relationships. The UM definition of religion was so broad as to overlap what most outsiders viewed as the secular, i.e., science, education, politics, and economics. For example, the UM as a religious organization violated the sharp boundaries between church and state by lobbying in Washington to foster anti-communism among federal leaders as part of its own struggle against Godless communism and by opposing former-President Nixon's removal from office during the Watergate scandal. Further, Moon's vision of a reformed world was essentially that of a socialist theocracy, which would have unified the political, religious and economic institutions.

Such a perspective alarmed the gatekeepers of the scientific, religious and political institution as it had required literally centuries of struggle to reach the delicately balanced accommodation of science and religion, on the one hand, and government and religion, on the other. Thus it is not surprising that Moon's vision for reasserting religious primacy provoked a series of governmental investigations probing activities alleged to be inappropriate to the group's religious status or potentially illegal.

Garnering sufficient *economic resources* to underwrite the vast social change envisioned by world-transforming movements poses a major problem for them. The necessities of amassing resources on a large scale, retaining members' full-time commitment to the pursuit of the movement's goals, and segregating them from the corrupting influence of the larger society generally push such movements toward an economic base that draws on the resources of the larger society without implicating members in that economic system. Operationally this implies techniques such as selling a highly valued, communally produced commodity or soliciting charitable donations. In either case, only highly ritualized encounters between members and outsiders were permitted, and both techniques were organized in such a way as to reinforce communal solidarity.

Since its membership for the most part lacked saleable skills or goods, the UM turned to solicitation for accruing financial resources. For a considerable part of at least their early years in the movement, members engaged in continuous "witnessing"/fund-rasing activity in areas of heavy human traffic and rapid turnover. This led to charges that the UM was interested solely in building a financial empire for its elite leaders, while masking their pecuniary ambitions under the guise of religion, and that they were exploiting naive individual members' labor and idealism for their own economic and political ends.

World-transforming movements anticipate imminent, cataclysmic social change as the old order is swept away and replaced by a new and better world. Further, such movements begin their awesome task with only a small coterie of followers. In order to enlarge rapidly the band of committed followers it is therefore necessary for the movement to *recruit members* from the larger society which it simultaneously condemns and relies upon for the raw material of the transformative process. The combination of imminent change, its cosmic significance and the sharp contrast between the evil of the present world and the purity of the new order makes it imperative that members commit themselves totally to the movement and segregate themselves from the corrupting influence of the larger society.

The UM's theology predicted world-transformation within members' lifetimes as mankind was restored to God's initial purpose. The tactics of recruitment and socialization upon which the UM relied reflected these exigencies. In order to build membership rapidly the UM directed its appeal to that group most receptive to idealistic causes, i.e., unattached young adults, and utilized recruitment/socialization techniques designed to effect swift "conversions" and intense commitment. Members resided in communal groups which both offered continuous emotional support and reinforcement and segregated them from all but highly ritualized contact with outsiders, including families. Indeed, the latter were replaced by a fictive kinship system in which UM leaders assumed parental roles, and members gave up conventional career and domestic aspirations for full-time pursuit of the UM's millennial goals. For most parents, who did not share either Moon's basic ideological premises or his visionary goals, their offsprings' personal sacrifices were seen as a tragic, pointless waste of their lives. Since for many individuals membership in the UM represented a sharp discontinuity with former lifestyles, parents were suspicious and apprehensive about the techniques used to produce these "apparent" conversions.

INSTITUTIONAL SOURCES OF THE ACM

Family. While the UM's pan-institutional orientation had significant implications for changing all institutions, it was the family and religion for which these implications were greatest. *The* institution most directly and significantly affected by the UM was the family. Indeed, since the UM defined man's original fall from grace as the failure of Adam and Eve to establish a God-centered family, the UM's theology was directed at creating spiritually perfect families which were to be the building blocks of the heavenly kingdom on earth. It was thus the focus of the communally organized groups referred to by members as "families" (in which members referred to each other as "brothers" and "sisters" and to Rev. and Mrs. Moon as "father" and "mother" respectively) to create the spiritual conditions for promoting the restoration of man to God. The primacy of the goal of achieving spiritual perfection elevated the UM "family" to a status above members' "fallen" biological families. At the least, UM members had relatively little time to spend with their biological families, and if the latter opposed UM members' commitments, members often were reluctantly forced to reject their biological families. The "loss" of families' young members to the UM and other religions was experienced at several levels.

First, as a world-transforming movement the UM required full-time commitment of its members, necessitating a communal lifestyle and wholesale abandonment of former careers, obligations, and associations, often including the biological family. Since the UM conducted missionary work throughout the country and even overseas, the physical separation of mobile members from their biological families was increased and prolonged.

Second, the consuming demands of the UM on members' energies and the revised priority of goals accepted in conversion left little time for frequent or regular communications with families. Further, the facts that members' worldviews had undergone profound change and that their day-to-day schedules displayed both uniformity and (from the families' perspectives) an alien rationale meant that there was little common ground in the content of communications. Even if members wished to keep up frequent communications with parents, it was a formidable task to convey either the details or the meaning of their own struggles for spiritual growth in their new lifestyle.

Third, the breach of reciprocity (at least from the parents' perspectives) implicit in the rejection and condemnation of their values and lifestyles contributed to their sense of "loss." Many parents had invested heavily in offspring, not simply in mundane economic terms but also in intangible emotional ways. While the specificity of parents' expectations for offsprings' careers varied, many parents looked forward to some vicarious pleasure from their childrens' accomplishments as they matured. The social embarrassment of having a child in a strange "cult," the confusion and hurt at being suddenly the object of his or her rejection and even outright scorn, further mixed with the persistent anxiety over his/her well-being, all combined to provide families with powerful motives to locate and restore young family members to their former lifestyles and values.

Despite the fact that many families felt a great sense of threat and outrage toward the movement, they lacked effective recourse within conventional institutional channels. In most cases the converts were legally adults, the parents having no legal right to dictate their offsprings' religious (or other) preferences and activities. Another obstacle confronting families was the unavailability of conventional mechanisms of social control due to the UM's status as a religious group. Distraught parents who turned to the police, district attorneys, state and national legislators, psychiatrists, and even clergy often received a sympathetic hearing but little concrete assistance within the confines of the law. Logistically, since individual family units were decentralized, there was no existing organizational structure through which they could act collectively. Indeed, most families originally viewed their problems as unique because they had not been in contact with other parents whose offspring had joined the UM or other groups and were unaware of the alleged organizational similarities of what they came to refer to as "cults." It was only after reading of similar instances in the press or accidental encounters between families in the same situation that they began to conceive of themselves as a group with common grievances.

Religion. Religion was the other institution for which the UM posed a serious challenge, for two major reasons. Most importantly, the movement's most highly developed resources were religious. The UM already possessed a credible, systematic and sophisticated theology in scriptural form. Thus the movement possessed the major resources necessary for mobilizing a radically sectarian religious movement within the Judeo-Christian tradition, such as a solution to theodicy (i.e., the problem of evil coexisting in a world created by an all-powerful God), a messianic figure possessing fresh revelations, and a scripture that extrapolated the ethical implications of these revelations.

Unlike individual family units, however, churches were part of already established formal networks (e.g., denominations; dioceses; city, regional, national, and international interfaith councils; cooperative missions organizations). Through these networks the religious institution was able to offer active, vociferous resistance to the UM. Since one element of the UM's mobilization strategy was to seek legitimation by attaching itself to the western Christian tradition, simply refusing to admit the UM to membership in such organizations (e.g., the National Council of Churches, the New York Council of Churches) undercut these efforts. Further, these networks of religious organizations provided a means of mobilizing opposition on the local level. For example, in the early 1970s during Sun Myung Moon's national speaking tours, various Christian groups ranging from fringe evangelical groups to mainline denominations banded together and served as important vehicles of communication concerning the itinerary of Moon's tours. As a result, Moon's entourage encountered noisy "welcoming committees" conducting demonstrations and other opposition activities, such as letters of protest in newspapers, pressures on owners of local facilities not to lease space to the UM for speaking engagements, and fiery denunciatory sermons. Religious leaders in some instances provided leadership to the ACM, (e.g., Rabbis Maurice Davis and James Rudin, Rev. George Swope, and Father Kent Burtner). These and other professionals, either out of direct personal involvement or sympathy, lent considerable credibility to the ACM by supporting its goals.

The religious institution, more than any other, was uniquely equipped to attack the UM's most basic source of legitimation: its theology. Moon's theology posed a direct challenge not only to virtually all American religious groups within the Judeo-Christian tradition but also to the pluralistic American religious tradition itself. American religion was a "closed fraternity" which admitted only these groups willing to abide by existing pluralistic ground rules of co-existence and limited competition. Moon's outspoken defense of his unificationist goals clearly located him outside this tradition; indeed, Moon unabashedly claimed as his mission the elimination of this pluralism and in its place the substitution of a monolithic theocracy. American churches in turn were well prepared to meet Moon's challenge by resisting his claims for legitimacy. Each denomination had once accommodated itself to the nation's pluralistic situation and had confronted the twin problems of schism and heresy. Thus established churches had already formulated categories of deviance which provided specific criteria for evaluating the authenticity of truth claims.

Finally, as acknowledged gatekeepers of moral and ethical education, churches could easily condemn Moon, his theology and his activities in the context of religious education. Leaders of a number of churches, such as those in the Lutheran Council in the USA (LCMP, 1977) and local chapters of the American Jewish Committee (AJC, 1979) prepared special "educational packets" on the "dangers of cults." These featured bibliographies of books and articles written from the traditional Judeo-Christian traditions, condemnations of "cults" by religious leaders, testimonies from former "cult" members, and even study guide/discussion questions for Sunday school teachers and youth leaders.

THE ACM AS A COUNTER-MOVEMENT

Organization. In the early 1970s parents typically became alarmed about their offsprings' new religious affiliations when they began to learn some of the details of the groups' ideologies and lifestyles. Ultimately parents levied charges of kidnapping or enslavement against the UM, but these became difficult to sustain when the alleged "victims" reaffirmed their voluntary participation in their faiths. In the process of expressing grievances to officials and media reporters, however, parents did become aware that they were not alone and that other parents were encountering problems with what sounded like similar groups and situations. It was at this point that families began to contact each other and meet to discuss their mutual problems.

Out of these contacts coalesced the first major ACM organization in 1972: The Parents' Committee to Free Our Sons and Daughters from the Children of God Organization, or FREECOG. For two years FREECOG resisted pressures to expand its concerns beyond merely the Children of God, but gradually, as "atrocity stories" about other groups' methods of indoctrination, fund-rasing tactics, and organizational styles began to accumulate, FREECOG members became convinced that there was a more general "cult" problem. Thus, in 1974 FREECOG expanded (after some organizational trial and error) into the Citizens Freedom Foundation which eventually became *the* major anti-cult organization in the western United States. Establishing a "working precedent" that was to become the pattern of ACM groups later, CFF members decided that in order not to spread their limited resources too thinly they ought to focus their attack on the most powerful, visible, and dangerous of the "cults," the UM (Personal Interviews, 1976). This same process by which CFF developed was repeated spontaneously across the continental United States as parents independently experienced the same problems and banded together in similar fashion. In the mid-1970's there was a proliferation of anti-cult groups, many surfacing for a time as autonomous entities, then dissolving or merging into larger groups or coalitions.[3]

By early 1976 sufficient national attention had been drawn to the "new" religions that local anti-cult groups had become aware of each other's presence and activities and began to coordinate their attacks on what they termed "cults." The first national manifestation of this alliance came in February, 1976, when over 400 ACM members met with Senator Robert Dole and other federal government officials at a public hearing in Washington to call for an investigation of the UM. One year later the six largest regional ACM groups merged into a single national coalition (the International Foundation for Individual Freedom), largely because it had achieved tax-exempt status as an educational foundation. The merger was never very successful, however, as regional groups were reluctant to relinquish their autonomy and identities, to disband their own leaderships and to pool resources. Internal divisions persisted and several months later the ACM returned to its former organizational state consisting of decentralized regional organizations.

These organizations served a number of functions for their members, such as monitoring the activities and locations of various new religious groups, providing expressive forums in which parents could share their mutual anxieties, and operating as clearinghouses of information for parents who had recently "lost" sons or daughters. But their primary organizational objectives always were twofold: (a) to *locate and "rescue"* the youth, and (b) to *discredit* the "cults." Even the latter goal was clearly ancillary to the former since discrediting the "cults," aside from motives of revenge and/or "public service," was chiefly perceived by all involved as a more indirect means of recovering their sons or daughters by destroying the "cults."

Ideology. Two overriding problems confronted the ACM in its crusade to oppose the "cults." First, a relatively small number of families were actually affected by the predicament of young persons joining such groups. In order to combat them effectively, therefore, it was necessary for the ACM to build public support for its own position and to mobilize opposition to the "cults." Second, as previously noted, most of the individuals involved in the "cults" were legally adults. Any overt actions which involved parents forcibly removing their offspring from these groups constituted at least abrogation of their civil rights, and potentially involved assault and kidnapping. Both to mobilize public and official opinion against the "cults" and to neutralize opposition to

---

[3] The names of these emerging regional organizations were expressive of their overriding goals: Citizens Engaged in Reuniting Families, Love Our Children, Return to Personal Choice, Citizens Organized for the Public Awareness of Cults, and the National Ad Hoc Committee Engaged in Freeing Minds.

quasi-legal or illegal activities by ACM members, the development of some legitimating ideology was imperative.

Like the ACM organizational structure, its ideology did not spring forth full grown but rather emerged in gradual, piecemeal fashion. In its mature form, which was crystallized by the mid-1970s, the ACM ideology was composed of the following four basic assumptions:

(a) The UM (and other "cults") were pseudo-religions which had adopted the cloak of religion solely to gain tax-exempt privileges and insulation from legal regulation. These pseudo-religions were, in reality, profit-making ventures operated by ego-manic charlatans for their own personal aggrandizement.

(b) The youths who innocently became involved in the UM did not undergo a true conversion but rather were victims of deceptive, seductive, and/or manipulative processes that destroyed their free will (labeled "mind control" or "brainwashing").

(c) The "programming" process and the resultant subjugation of members was considered both physically and mentally deleterious to them. In addition, the purposes for which these "automatons" were used were socially injurious to a number of institutions (e.g., family, Judeo-Christian religion, and American democracy).

(d) Since the free will of members had been suspended by the "programming" process, they were considered incapable of voluntarily leaving these groups; hence the only hope for their reassuming conventional lifestyles was to "deprogram" them.[4]

This ideology served to solve the two major problems of the ACM. First, it was possible to present to the media a seemingly coherent explanation, couched in behavioral science jargon, which identified a real social problem and not merely a personal domestic dispute. There existed a body of psychological research based on Korea War POW's experiences (Lifton, 1957, 1963; Hunter, 1953, 1962) as well as more popularized interpretations of these findings (Sargent, 1957; Merloo, 1956) that seemed to corroborate their claims. Second, the incapacitation presumed by the brainwashing model moved the individuals so labeled from the category of self-determining adults into that of helpless dependents. This imagery, when accepted, lowered public and official resistance to otherwise questionable or illegal activities by ACM members designed to recover their offspring. In fact, the ACM was extremely successful in disseminating its programming/deprogramming ideology, as witnessed by the literally thousands of "atrocity stories" about the UM that

---

[4] Deprogramming actually referred to a variety of activities ranging from discussions with parents over the telephone to the much publicized kidnapping/internment accompanied by inquisitional treatment, but it was the latter only which came to be publicly thought of as deprogramming.

were uncritically reported by the media (Bromley, Shupe and Ventimiglia, 1979).

Strategy and Tactics. Given the primacy of recovering sons or daughters from the UM as an ACM goal, it might be supposed that deprogramming would have played a prominent role in ACM strategy. In fact this did not occur, for several reasons. First, attempts to vest these recoveries with the "color of law" were largely unsuccessful. Early in the 1970s a number of parents and "professional" deprogrammers were able to seize UM members and subject them to coercive reconversion measures with the sympathetic non-interference of police and judiciaries. But by the mid-1970s UM members, financed by the movement, began to initiate legal action in the form of injunctions, lawsuits, and criminal prosecutions. A related tactic, that of ACM members attempting to have UM members awarded to their custody under the provisions of temporary conservatorship laws, was successfully employed only in a handful of cases and for a brief period before a series of precedent-setting court cases virtually eliminated this possibility. Second, the economic cost of deprogramming was prohibitive. The cost of locating the individuals, often across great distances, investigators' fees, legal costs, deprogrammers' fees, and so forth put this tactic out of reach for all but affluent families, particularly in light of their mixed successes. Third, while many families were genuinely distressed at their offsprings' choice of lifestyle, they were reluctant to coerce their sons and daughters or to subject them to the control of strangers about whom unsavory stories gradually began to circulate. Of course, parents continued to try to dissuade their offspring from continuing their UM affili-ations, but most restricted their activities to less heavy-handed tactics. Many simply hoped to wait out this period of youthful experimentation.

Since so many factors worked to discourage deprogrammings and related activities, the ACM devoted most of its resources to discrediting the "cults" via more conventional means and soliciting the assistance of leaders of other institutional sectors who had more effective social control mechanisms at their disposal. The ACM itself launched a series of "educational" campaigns, contacting church organizations, PTAs, chambers of commerce, newspapers, local businesses and other civic groups in attempts to cut off any unwitting cooperation with the UM. For example, school children were warned of the dangers of "cults," businessmen were asked to prohibit UM solicitation on their premises, and media were requested to warn citizens whenever UM witnessing or fund-raising teams appeared in the locale.

Beyond its own campaigns, the ACM sought assistance from several other institutions. The most prominent example was an extensive lobbying campaign directed at congressmen and the heads of certain governmental agencies (e.g., the Internal Revenue Service, the Immigration and Naturalization Service). In

1977, for example, the national ACM coalition mounted an extensive campaign to have a UM official cited for contempt of Congress for refusing to testify before the "Fraser Committee" (the House Subcommittee on International Organizations, chaired by Rep. Donald E. Fraser). To this end a professional lobbyist was retained for several visits to congressmen, and ACM members across the country participated in a letter-writing campaign to their representatives. In 1978, a similar letter-writing campaign was conducted to generate support for an anti-cult resolution under consideration by the national PTA at its annual convention. In many cases, local ACM groups lobbied to prevent the UM college organization C.A.R.P. (Collegiate Association for the Research of Principles) from opening chapters on college campuses.

The combination of tactics employed by the ACM began to take its toll on the UM by the mid-1970s. The ACM's persistent publicity campaign succeeded in creating an extremely negative image of the UM in the media as a strange and dangerous cult. As a consequence, UM witnessing and fund-raising teams consistently encountered hostility and opposition in local communities across the country, and communities regularly banded together to prevent the establishment of UM centers or enterprises in their locales. The ACM's intensive lobbying efforts aimed at political, educational and religious leaders resulted in the UM's being denied legitimacy by gatekeepers of a number of established institutions. For example, the Unification Theological Seminary was denied accreditation by the New York State Board of Regents, local governmental officials employed solicitation ordinances to prevent the UM from fund-raising, despite the unconstitutionality of such ordinances, and the National Council of Churches denied the UM membership. Deprogramming also had a more serious impact on the UM than the number of members deprogrammed might suggest. The constant threat of abduction created an atmosphere of defensiveness and distrust; members were wary of returning home for visits, were reluctant to comply with requests to identify themselves as fund-raisers for fear of having their identities passed on to ACM leaders, and sometimes moved about without notifying their families in order to avoid detection. Of course "successful deprogrammings" also hurt morale. It was understandably disheartening for members to hear of former co-workers and friends condemning them and the UM's goals or to read of their idealistic motives called into question and their venerated leader slandered. Moreover, these cases were major symbolic defeats for the UM in that they buttressed the "deprogramming" model and "proved" that this extremist tactic worked.

Summary and Conclusions

We have examined the institutional origin, composition, and operation of the ACM as a counter-movement directed against the UM in particular and new religous groups of the world-transforming type in general. As we have seen, the ACM emerged in response to the specific characteristics of world transforming movements like the UM. Those institutions which spearheaded the ACM, the family and religion, were the ones most directly affected by the UM and other similar movements. The ACM's organizational structure, ideology and tactics can be understood as flowing from the impact of the UM's mobilization on them and from their two major goals of rescuing the "innocent victims" of cults and discrediting or destroying the cults themselves. Through the latter 1970s the ACM's tactics were relatively successful: the UM's public image was extremely negative, the movement was no closer to "unifying" either America's pluralistic religions or its other institutions, and the UM was continually embroiled in controversy with gatekeepers of the political, religious, educational, and economic institutions.

REFERENCES

AJC (American Jewish Committee). 1979. Study Guide on Religious Cults. Dallas: Dallas Chapter, American Jewish Committee.

Anthony, D., and T. Robbins. 1974. "The Meher Baba movement: its effect on post-adolescent social alienation." In I. I. Zaretsky and M.P. Leone (eds.), *Religious Movements in Contemporary America*. Princeton: Princeton University.

Bromley, D. G., and A. D. Shupe, Jr.. 1979a. "Moonies" in America: Cult, Church, and Crusade. Beverly Hills: Sage..

1979b. "'Just a few years seem like a lifetime': a role theory approach to participation in religious movements." In L. Kriesberg (ed.), *Research in Social Movements, Conflict and Change*. Greenwich, Conn.: Jai Press.

1979c. "Evolving foci in participant observation: research as an emerging process." In W. Shaffir, A. Turowitz and R. Stebbins (eds.), *The Social Experience of Field Work*. New York: St. Martin's.

Bromley, D. G., A. D. Shupe, Jr., and J. C. Ventimiglia. 1979. "The role of anecdotal atrocities in the social construction of evil." Paper presented at the Annual Meeting of the American Sociological Association, Boston.

Danner, F. 1976. The American Children of KRSNA. Dallas: Holt, Rinehart and Winston.

Enroth, R. 1977. "Cult/countercult." *Eternity:* 19-22,32-5.

Gamson, W. A. 1975. The Strategy of Social Protest. Homewood, Ill.: Dorsey.

Glock, C. Y., and R. N. Bellah (eds.). 1976. The New Religious Consciousness. Berkeley: University of California.

Hunter, E. 1953. Brainwashing in Red China: The Calculated Destruction of Men's Minds. New York: Vanguard.

1962. Brainwashing: From Pavlov to Powers. New York: The Bookmailer.

Lifton, R. J. 1957. "Thought reform of Chinese intellectuals: a psychiatric evaluation." *Journal of Social Issues* 13: 5-20.

1963. Thought Reform and the Psychology of Totalism. New York: Norton.

LCMP (Lutheran Campus Ministries Program). 1977. The Cults: A Resource Packet. Chicago: Lutheran Council in the USA.

Lofland, J. 1977. Doomsday Cult (Enlarged Edition). New York: Irvington.

McCarthy, J., and M. N. Zald. 1973. The Trend of Social Movements in America: Professionalization and Resource Mobilization. Morristown: General Learning Press.

1974. "Tactical considerations in social movement organizations." Paper presented at the Annual Meeting of the American Sociological Association, Montreal.

1977. "Resource mobilization in social movements: a partial theory." American Journal of Sociology 82: 1212-39.

Merloo, J. 1956. The Rape of the Mind. New York: World.

Needleman, J., and G. Baker (eds.). 1978. Understanding the New Religions. New York: Seabury.

Richardson, J. T. (ed.). 1978. Conversion Careers: In and Out of New Religious Groups. Beverly Hills: Sage.

Robbins, T., D. Anthony, and J. T. Richardson. 1978. "Theory and research on today's 'new religions'." Sociological Analysis 39: 95-122.

Sargent, W. 1957. Battle for the Mind. New York: Doubleday.

Shupe, A. D., Jr., and D. G. Bromley. 1978. "Some continuities in American religion: witches, moonies and accusations of evil." Paper presented at the Annual Meeting of the Association for the Scientific Study of Religion, Southwest.

1980a. The New Vigilantes: Deprogrammers, Anti-Cultists, and the New Religions. Beverly Hills: Sage.

1980b. "Walking a tightrope; participant observation among groups in conflict." Qualitative Sociology, Forthcoming.

Shupe, A. D., Jr., R. Spielmann, and S. Stigall. 1977a. "Deprogramming and the emerging American anti-cult movement." Paper presented at the Annual Meeting of the Society for the Scientific Study of Religion, Chicago.

1977b. "Deprogramming: the new exorcism." American Behavioral Scientist 20: 941-56.

Wallis, R. 1977. The Road to Total Freedom. New York: Columbia University.

Zald, M. N., and R. Ash. 1973. "Social movement organizations: growth, decay, and change." In R. R. Evans (ed.), Social Movements: A Reader and Source Book. Chicago: Rand McNally.

Zald, M. N., and M. A. Berger. 1978. "Social movements in organizations: coup d'etat, insurgency, and mass movements." American Journal of Sociology 83: 823-61.

Zaretsky, I., and M. P. Leone (eds.). 1974. Religious Movements in Contemporary America. Princeton: Princeton University.

III

New Politics

JUST as the spread of new religions highlighted the 1970s, the new political activism of conservative Protestants bids to dominate religious headlines in the 1980s. That development is no less surprising than the cult explosion, and at least as controversial. It was barely a decade ago that this wing of Protestantism was denouncing anti-war clerics and earlier, civil rights demonstrators, for abandoning the church's mission of saving souls for social action. Conservative Christians remain strongly opposed to established "liberal" culture, but now they are doing something about it. And since evangelicals have entered the political wars in earnest, liberals have sounded the alarm about free speech and the separation of church and state.

Its parallels with new religions notwithstanding, the evangelical resurgence is distinctive in two important ways. First, while most new religions followed a centrifugal course away from society, the new religious politics is a centripetal social force, leading the sacred back toward the organizational center of modern society. There preachers consort with presidents, not for nondenominational prayer breakfasts but to discuss political issues, aims and strategies, and to bask in each other's limelight. Second, the evangelicals bring substantial resources to their task, chief among which is their ability to communicate and mobilize supporters through the mass media, the modern substitute for precinct captains. In sum, the new Christian right is a very potent force which cannot be dismissed as a reactionary movement of little long-term significance.

Before we can gauge what that power will mean for religion and society however, we need to know what people are doing with it and why. If that sounds simple, consider the three papers in this section. The first of them ("Sounds of Silence Revisited") by Norman Koller and Joseph Retzer attempts to correct a long-standing mistake. "Sounds of Silence" was the title of a pop magazine version of a Stark et. al. study of California clergy conducted in the late 1960s. That title crystallized their finding that clergy, especially conservative ones, failed to preach on controversial social issues. A decade after all the political turmoil of the late 1960s, Koller and Retzer found that North Carolina ministers, contrary to the silence of California clergy, were preaching on all sorts of controversial social issues. Unfortunately, Koller and Retzer did not ask clergy what they had to say, but we may infer that as theologically conservative ministers, they were likely preaching politically conservative messages. If this inference is correct, the Koller and Retzer findings are consistent with an Indianapolis study by James Wood. He found that laity don't at all object to the clergy's speaking on social issues so long as the ministers' view parallel their own.

Louise Lorentzen's task was to find out what happened to an early evangelical electoral effort before the phenomenon vanished. In the Spring of 1978, a car dealer and city councillor from an eastern Virginia city felt God had called him to seek the Democratic Party's nomination for the U. S. Senate. In just two months, Conoly Phillips garnered 330 convention delegates and ran third in a large field of candidates, many of whom had been campaigning for well over a year. Lorentzen interviewed the convention delegates from one Virginia city and one country as well as a random sample of mass meeting participants to find out what drew persons who traditionally have been apolitical into the political arena. Drawing upon Weber's idea of "status politics," she found evangelicals' moving into politics was a way of symbolizing their commitment to a life style at odds with the dominant character of American life. In 1978 the rapid movement of evangelicals onto (and off) the political scene seemed almost quixotic. Today their crusades are no longer just symbolic, but Lorentzen's early account of why they do it still rings true.

In the emotional world of religious politics, stereotypes, prejudice and misinformation abound. Hadden's paper on "Televangelism and the New Christian Right" attempts to correct some of those errors and to set straight the story of TV preachers' recent involvement in politics. Elaborating on his recent study of *Prime-Time Preachers,* he shows that most people either take the new politics too seriously or not seriously enough. In the former camp are those who believe evangelicals will turn our country into a religious dictatorship. Among the latter are those who still suspect they are a passing fad. Hadden reminds us that the evangelical tradition is longstanding in American life and suggests that it will become an even more important social force now that it has the power of telecommunication and computerized fund-raising. At the same time, Hadden indicates how loosely organized this political force actually is. Numerous organizations and publications compete for the public's loyalty, TV preachers are notoriously independent operators, and there is no consensus of political belief on specific issues. More than political platforms, it is the drift of culture which concerns Christians on the right. Politics is the current outlet for that concern, but that effort to reshape America may take different forms in the future.

5

THE SOUNDS OF SILENCE REVISITED

Norman B. Koller, Joseph D. Retzer

INTRODUCTION

In 1971, Rodney Stark *et al.*, published *Wayward Shepherds,* a study of clergy, their attitudes toward controversial social and political issues, and their preaching on these topics in the late 1960s. Some of their major findings were earlier summarized in an article entitled "Sounds of Silence" (Stark *et al.,* 1970). The research team concluded that, in spite of the heated political and social climate of the time, most clergy were reluctant to speak out on controversial issues. Further, ministers in doctrinally conservative denominations were the least likely to address social issues. As the titles of the article and book imply, Stark and his colleagues assigned a status of moral superiority to clergy who raised their voices in indignation against social injustices. This bias permeates much of their analysis both overtly and subtly.

The purpose of this paper is to re-examine the central findings of Stark *et al.,* especially those relating to differences between "liberal" and "conservative" clergy. The study from which it is developed differs from the Stark *et al.* study in two important respects. First, it reflects clergy opinion and action ten years later. The late 1960s were characterized by loud voices of protest against all sorts of injustice. Stark *et al.* even called 1968 "one of the most agonizing years in American history" (Stark *et al.,* 1971:90). In sharp contrast, the late 1970s have been described as a period of quiet desperation and acquiescence to much which seemed beyond control of the average person. This dramatic shift in cultural mood might be expected to have an important impact on the reaction of clergy to social issues. A second important difference is that whereas the Stark survey was conducted in California, noted for its liberal views, this study was conducted in North Carolina. If these differences place serious limitations on our ability to replicate directly the earlier study, they also provide interesting opportunities for comparative speculation.

METHODOLOGY

A questionnaire was mailed to 468 Protestant ministers in a two-county area of southwestern North Carolina in the spring of 1978.[1] Follow-up phone calls and post cards netted 232 useable questionnaires, or a response rate of 49.6 percent. Returns by denomination ranged from 75 percent for Episcopalians to 46 percent for Baptists, with the residual category "other" returning only 39 percent.[2] Data obtained included self-reported theological and political views, age, Likert-type items measuring attitudes toward social and political issues, and a battery of twenty items designed to ascertain what social and political topics, if any, these clergy had dealt with in sermons during the previous year. In addition, the questionnaire asked about the size and estimated SES of each minister's congregation.

The major independent variable in this study is *doctrinal orthodoxy,* measured by a six item index which closely parallels a similar index developed and widely used by Charles Glock and Rodney Stark (Stark *et al.,* 1971:26). The items cover belief in the (1) existence of a personal God, (2) divinity of Jesus, (3) existence of the devil, (4) life after death, (5) Jesus walking on water, and (6) virgin birth. For each item, the respondent may affirm a range of views from literal belief in scriptures to doubt and disbelief.

The Doctrinal Orthodoxy Index yields a range of scores from six to twenty-one. The lower the score, the more literal or traditionally conservative the beliefs of the respondent. Nearly two-thirds (64%) of the clergy in our study gave the most orthodox responses to all six items in the index. In subsequent discussion, the concept "conservative" will be used interchangeably with "orthodox" or "doctrinally orthodox" to refer to this group. The concept "liberal" will be used to refer to all those who show any degree of deviation from literal Christian belief as measured by the Doctrinal Orthodoxy Index.[3]

Stark and his colleagues used two measures to analyze the extent of clergy discussion of controversial social and political topics from the pulpit. They asked first how many sermons "touched upon" selected topics and, second,

[1]The mailing list was secured from telephone directories. Non-Protestant religious leaders constituted less than five percent of all listings. They were excluded from this study because they constituted a group too small for systematic comparative analysis. The two counties studied were Iredell and Mecklenburg. The latter includes Charlotte, the state's largest metropolitan area.

[2]Further details on sampling and return rates by denomination may be obtained by writing to the senior author.

[3]This high level of Doctrinal Orthodoxy contrasts sharply with the California sample where only 38 percent expressed literal views on all six belief items. Differences in the two samples is also vividly revealed by examining individual items. For example, whereas only 50 percent of the California sample believed the statement "Jesus was born of a virgin" to be "literally true," nearly three-quarters (72%) of the North Carolina ministers did. And while 79 percent of the California ministers believe in a literal "life beyond death," 93 percent of the Carolina clergy do.

how many sermons "dealt mainly with" such topics. Clearly, the latter is the more demanding measure. It seems reasonable to expect that a minister might more likely merely mention rather than develop a whole sermon around a particular social or political theme. Indeed, this is what Stark *et al.* found. Nearly two-thirds of all clergy in their sample had touched upon controversial subjects. Yet, much of the analysis presented in *Wayward Shepherds* is based on the more demanding criterion of "dealt mainly with." By this criterion, the doctrinally orthodox in the California study were substantially less likely than were liberals to speak out on controversial issues. But when the data are examined using the criterion of merely touching upon a topic, the differences between "conservatives" and "liberals" are significantly reduced.

This observation suggested to us that conservative clergy may not be less concerned with social issues, but rather that they may approach such topics in a different "style." Whether because of theology or some other factor, the doctrinally conservative may differ systematically from the theologically liberal in *how* they deal with controversial topics. In order to test this proposition, the current study endeavored to examine the degree of attention devoted to various social issues. For each of twenty social issues, we asked clergy to indicate whether during the past year they had dealt with the topic as "a major theme," "a major point," "touched upon," or "not mentioned."

LEVEL OF INTEREST AND INVOLVEMENT IN SOCIAL AND POLITICAL QUESTIONS

Nearly all respondents expressed a high level of interest in social and political issues. Ninety-four percent agreed with the statement, "I am very interested in the contemporary social and political issues in current American society." Only a single minister out of 232 disagreed with the proposition that clergy have "a special obligation to stay politically informed," and four out of five (80%) felt they were "well informed" on major social and political issues.

In considering the clergy's role in social issues, 84 percent reported that their theological training encouraged them to speak out on social and political issues. Ninety percent felt it to be their "duty" to speak out in the *community*, and fully 82 percent felt they should do so in *sermons*. This distinction produced a lively commentary in the margins of questionnaires. Many clergy felt they should seek forums other than the pulpit to address social issues so as to minimize the prospects of creating controversy and divisiveness within congregations.

Table I summarizes the responses of the North Carolina clergy to twenty items asking the degree to which they addressed social and political issues from

TABLE 1

ATTENTION DEVOTED TO SOCIAL AND POLITICAL
ISSUES IN SERMONS DURING PREVIOUS YEAR

Topic	*Percent for Whom Topic Was:*				
	A Major Theme	*A Major Point*	*Touched Upon*	*Not Mentioned*	*Major Theme Plus Major Point*
Racial Problems	16%	39%	37%	8%	55%
World Poverty	13%	42%	34%	11%	55%
Crime or Juvenile Delinquency	13%	35%	38%	14%	48%
Energy/Environmental Crisis	12%	35%	37%	16%	47%
National Poverty	12%	33%	41%	13%	45%
Conduct of Public Officials	8%	37%	44%	11%	45%
Sex or Violence on TV	7%	38%	41%	14%	45%
Control of Drug Abuse	10%	32%	43%	15%	42%
The Middle East Situation	9%	26%	50%	16%	35%
Capital Punishment	9%	25%	40%	26%	34%
Inflation or Unemployment	5%	25%	49%	21%	30%
Pornography	5%	21%	45%	29%	26%
Prayer/Religion in the Schools	8%	18%	40%	34%	26%
Abortion Laws	4%	21%	36%	39%	25%
The Equal Rights Amendment	6%	17%	48%	29%	23%
Communism	5%	14%	42%	39%	19%
Liquor by the Drink	4%	14%	40%	42%	18%
Sex Education in the Schools	4%	12%	38%	45%	16%
The Wilmington Ten Case	3%	10%	25%	61%	13%
Labor/Management Relations	0	12%	50%	37%	12%

the pulpit during the year prior to the study. Leading the list of topics discussed from the pulpit were racial problems and world poverty. Fifty-five percent of our respondents said that each of these subjects was dealt with either as a major point or a major theme in sermons. In addition, slightly more than a third said they had touched upon these topics. Five additional topics provided a major point or theme for 45 percent or more of the clergy in the study; these included "crime or juvenile delinquency," the "energy/environmental crisis," "national poverty," the "conduct of public officials," and "sex or violence on television." In addition, "drug abuse," the "Middle-East crisis," and "capital punishment" were topics of major concern for more than a third of the clergy. Note also in Table I that the proportion of clergy reporting that they at least touched upon topics is considerable.

In short, these data suggest that North Carolina clergy are rather vocal on social and political issues. This conclusion is reinforced by comparison with the California study. Only thirteen percent of the North Carolina ministers indicated they had not mentioned *any* of the twenty social issues on our list. By contrast, fully 25 percent of the California sample did not address any of the social issues raised by Stark and his colleagues. Furthermore, more than nine out of ten North Carolina ministers (93%) answered affirmatively the question of whether they had *ever taken a stand* on a political issue from the pulpit. In rather sharp contrast, only 62 percent of the California clergy reported having done so.

DOCTRINALISM AND OTHER-WORLDLINESS AS SOURCES OF SILENCE

Stark and his colleagues accounted for differences in the frequency of speaking out from the pulpit in theological terms. They reported a "very strong" and positive relationship between doctrinal orthodoxy and silence on social and political issues. Given the high proportion of ministers in our sample who scored high on doctrinal orthodoxy and their relatively higher level of speaking out on social issues, we would be surprised if our data supported the Stark *et al.* findings. They do not. Dichotomizing our sample into "high" and "low" based on a total score for each minister on the twenty social issues, we found essentially no difference between conservatives and liberals in their propensity to address social issues. Forty-eight percent of those scoring high on the Doctrinal Orthodoxy Index compared with 49 percent of the balance of the sample scored high on "speaking out."

Stark *et al.* argued that doctrinal conservatives were silent on social issues because "they believe salvation of the individual is the only relevant solution to such problems" (Stark *et al.*, 1971:128). In support of this argument they asked clergy three questions designed to measure "other-worldliness." By this measure, they found a strong correlation between other worldly responses and both doctrinal orthodoxy and silence from the pulpit on political issues. Again, our findings fail to support this. We found those who scored high on "speaking out'' were slightly more likely to select this-worldly as compared to other-worldly responses to the questions.[4]

THEOLOGICAL ORIENTATION AND TYPE OF ISSUES

We have seen that overall scores for speaking out on social and political issues were not significantly different for orthodox and liberal clergy. We might expect, however, that these two groups would tend to focus on different types of issues. Stark *et al.* argue that when conservative clergy do speak out they tend to focus on "personal vices" and "individualistic morality." They report, for example, that drugs, alcoholism, sexual conduct, and crime drew substantial pulpit discussion from doctrinally conservative ministers.

Table 2 examines responses to the twenty topics by liberal and conservative clergy in our sample. The data are rank ordered according to the frequency with which the topics were a "major theme" or a "major point" for liberal clergy. The proportion of conservative clergy treating these topics as a major point or theme is also presented, with rank order in parentheses. The right hand column presents the percentage differences between liberals and conservatives who developed each issue in sermons.

Our first observation is that liberal ministers appear closer to consensus on what the major social issues are. Four issues emerged as major themes or points for nearly two-thirds or more of liberal clergy. These topics were world poverty (76%), race problems (70%), national poverty (65%) and the energy crisis (65%).

Significantly fewer of the doctrinally orthodox clergy devoted major attention to these topics in their sermons: between one-fourth and one-third in contrast to roughly two-thirds of the liberal clergy. The top four social issues for conservatives were crime (50%), sex and violence on TV (49%), race problems (46%), and drug abuse (44%). On the face of it, these findings seem to support the interpretation of Stark and his colleagues that liberal ministers are concerned with major social structure issues and conservatives are preoccupied with personal vices or sins. Such an interpretation, we believe, is a serious misreading of the data.

First, the conservative clergy tend on average to give attention to a broader range of topics than do the liberal clergy. Almost half of the twenty topics (nine) failed to receive major consideration in the sermons of three-quarters of

[4]The three items used by Stark *et al.* and replicated in this study were as follows: "It would be better if the church were to place less emphasis on individual sanctification and more on bringing human conditions into conformity with Christian teachings" (*this-worldly*); "If enough men were brought to Christ, social ills would take care of themselves" (*other-worldly*); and "It is not as important to worry about life after death as about what one can do in this life" (*this-worldly*). Data on the responses of clergy to these items may be obtained by writing to the senior author.

the liberal clergy. In contrast, only three of the twenty topics failed to capture the attention of fewer than one-quarter of the orthodox ministers. Moreover, of the ten most frequently developed sermon topics, nine were common to liberals and conservatives.

We interpret the data to suggest a tendency for the doctrinally orthodox to focus on the interplay between public laws and protection of the community from influences they believe to be immoral. There appears to be an emphasis

TABLE 2

SERMONS DEALING WITH SOCIAL ISSUES
BY THEOLOGICAL ORIENTATION OF CLERGY

	THEOLOGICAL ORIENTATIONS				
	LIBERALS % Giving Topic As Major Theme or Point	Rank	CONSERVATIVES % Giving Topic As Major Theme or Point	Rank	% Difference Between Liberals and
SERMON TOPICS	in Sermon	Order	in Sermon	Order	Conservatives
World Poverty	76%	(1)	43%	(5)	+33
Race Problems	70%	(2)	46%	(3)	+24
National Poverty	65%	(3)	33%	(10)	+32
Energy Crisis	65%	(4)	36%	(7)	+29
Conduct of Public Officials	51%	(5)	41%	(6)	+10
Crime	43%	(6)	50%	(1)	−7
Capital Punishment	42%	(7)	29%	(13)	+13
Middle East	37%	(8)	34%	(9)	+3
Sex or Violence on TV	36%	(9)	49%	(2)	−13
Drug Abuse	36%	(10)	44%	(4)	−8
Inflation	34%	(11)	26%	(14)	+8
Wilmington Ten	24%	(12)	7%	(20)	+17
ERA	20%	(13)	25%	(16)	−5
Pornography	16%	(14)	31%	(11)	−15
Labor Relations	16%	(15)	10%	(19)	+6
Abortion	15%	(16)	30%	(12)	−15
Sex Education	12%	(17)	19%	(18)	−7
Prayer in the Schools	11%	(18)	34%	(8)	−23
Communism	7%	(19)	26%	(15)	−19
Liquor	4%	(20)	24%	(17)	−20

on nurturing the spiritual side of life by maintaining or creating a social order which enhances individual opportunity to lead a "spiritually upright" and "morally correct" existence. From this perspective, proper social order should minimize temptations to stray from the straight and narrow path (opposition to pornography, liquor by the drink, and sex and violence on TV); provide moral guidance for the young (protection of school religious education); and avoid legalizing or rewarding immoral acts (opposition to abortion and "coddling" of criminals).

In contrast, liberal ministers concentrate on issues involving physical life conditions of various segments of the community. Poverty, the energy crisis, and racial problems have less to do with spiritual growth than with ministering to the economic needs of the community's poorest members.

This distinction is subtly but distinctively different from the "other-worldy—this-worldly," and "private vice—public issue" dichotomies suggested by Stark *et al*. Their conclusion is that doctrinally orthodox ministers are concerned almost exclusively with private relations between man and God and, thus, are not interested in "worldly" social and political issues as sermon topics. Our interpretation suggests that concern for private man-God relationships promotes interest in particular types of public issues. Principally the doctrinally orthodox are concerned with public issues that relate to providing a social order in which the possibility of leading a morally upright life is enhanced.

This difference in orientation toward social issues may not be altogether pleasing to Stark and his colleagues who seem clearly to prefer those who choose to express their religious convictions by more or less direct engagement in solving social problems. But it is an honest difference grounded in theological orientation. It is a difference among honorable persons, parallel in some respects to differences about how best to curb inflation, stimulate the economy, etc. No one knows the answers with empirical certainty. But whether we are talking about the economy or social issues, orientation to how best to address the topics is ultimately grounded in ideology and faith. And as sociologists, our task should be to understand what people believe and how they are motivated, not to order and sort them in terms of the coincidence of their beliefs with our own.

CONCLUSIONS

Using a Southern sample to re-examine the Stark *et al*. study of involvement in social and political issues via the pulpit, we found two major areas of disagreement. First, we found much higher levels of attention devoted to social issues in sermons in 1978 than Stark and his colleagues reported for 1968.

Second, we found doctrinal orthodoxy to be a poor predictor of who speaks out on social issues. The temporal and regional differences in these two studies make direct comparability impossible. However, we feel that some speculative effort to account for the differences can both enhance our understanding and help focus the attention and direction of future investigations.

We would suggest that two factors are probably of major importance. First, it appears that the Stark *et al.* approach to measuring the degree to which clergy address social and political issues from the pulpit underestimates the actual amount. Their own published data suggest they might have evolved rather different interpretations had they not chosen to concentrate their analysis on those who preached sermons dealing "mainly" with controversial topics. In doing so, they essentially excluded from analysis the thoughts of more ortho-dox clergy who addressed social issues but tended not to make these topics the major focus of their sermons. Our data suggest that giving respondents a broader range of response categories does increase response variance.

A second major factor accounting for the divergent findings may indeed be regional. The cultural and political setting of North Carolina may be more conducive to active political concern for doctrinally orthodox religious leaders than is California. In North Carolina, as in much of the South, religion is a significant part of the culture, and the dominant churches are doctrinally orthodox, especially the Baptists. Ministers of this conservative Protestant denomination historically have been active in issue-oriented campaigns in the state, frequently being a deciding element in political struggles.

It may be of some importance to note that neither this study nor Stark's ascertained information on *what* clergy had to say about the various social and political issues they addressed. Stark and his colleagues seem to infer that clergy who speak out do so with a liberal voice. This assumption may not be al-together valid. Hadden (1969), among others, found significant correlations between theological and political beliefs. Thus, we might expect theologically conservative clergy to hold conservative viewpoints as to how to deal with the social and political issues in question. If we further assume that their congrega-tions tend to be both theologically and politically conservative, it is reasonable to speculate that sermonizing on these topics would not lead to as great a controversy among members of their congregations as would be the case in "mainline" or liberal Protestant traditions where a broader spectrum of social and political ideology is present.

Following this line of reasoning, one might wish to reexamine Stark's assumption that high levels of controversy and social conflict are a stimulus to pulpit discussion of social issues. It would seem equally plausible that the great volatility of social and political issues during the late 1960s may have had the reverse effect from that suggested by Stark *et al.* Furthermore, the stifling effect may have been greater for conservative ministers in the liberal California milieu.

Whether our explanations provide plausible accounts for the differences between the two studies will have to be judged by others. What should not be lost sight of by those who may disagree with our interpretations is that clergy in the deep South were significantly more vocal on social issues from the pulpit in 1978 than were clergy in liberal California in 1968 near the very height of social activism among clergy in America. This finding, we feel, cries out for more systematic research and further interpretation.

REFERENCES

Hadden, Jeffrey K. 1969. The Gathering Storm in the Churches. Garden City, New York: Doubleday.

Stark, Rodney, *et al*. 1970. ''The Sounds of Silence.'' *Psychology Today 3* (April).

Stark, Rodney, *et al*. 1971. Wayward Shepherds. New York: Harper and Row.

6

EVANGELICAL LIFE STYLE CONCERNS EXPRESSED IN POLITICAL ACTION

Louise J. Lorentzen

INTRODUCTION

During the past half century, the majority of evangelical Christians have remained theologically and socially conservative and, with few exceptions, politically uninvolved. Their traditional approach to alleviating social problems has been evangelism aimed at individual regeneration rather than political action aimed at structural change. Although appeals for involvement in the political process have come from highly visible evangelicals, seldom have they stirred a participant audience. Only in the past decade, some indications of activism have emerged among a small minority of evangelicals who affirm a more liberal theology and life style (Gerstner, 1975; Linder, 1975; Marsden, 1975; Moberg, 1972; Pierard, 1970; Quebedeaux, 1978).

In this context, the race for the 1978 Democratic nomination for a U.S. Senate seat from Virginia is of considerable interest. This race was marked by the unprecedented involvement of evangelical Christians in Virginia state politics. In all, eight aspirants contended for the support of 2,795 convention delegates chosen at local mass meetings throughout the state. One of these aspirants, an evangelical Christian, was a newcomer to state politics and the Democratic party who announced his candidacy for the nomination only eight weeks before the mass meetings. Yet, in that brief time, he was able to secure 330 convention delegates, placing him third in the bid for the nomination. This 12 percent of the total number of delegates fell far short of establishing this evangelical candidate as a viable contender for the nomination. However, the relative success of his campaign is noteworthy because of (1) the brevity of the campaign effort, (2) the unique appeal based on the candidate's character and reputation as a Christian leader rather than his position on specific political issues, (3) the open solicitation of support from the ranks of evangelical church

TABLE 1

SUMMARY RESULTS OF VIRGINIA DELEGATE SURVEY*
DELEGATE POSITION ON ISSUES OF LIFE STYLE AND MORALITY

Issue	Favor (%)	Oppose (%)	Undecided (%)
Equal Rights Amendment			
Republicans	21	70	9
Democrats (excluding evangelical delegates)	66	24	10
Evangelical Candidate Delegates	4	90	6
Death Penalty for First Degree Murder			
Republicans	73	11	16
Democrats (excluding evangelical delegates)	38	45	17
Evangelical Candidate Delegates	55	18	27
Decriminalization of Marijuana			
Republicans	26	59	16
Democrats (excluding evangelical delegates)	54	30	16
Evangelical Candidate Delegates	7	87	6
Abortion Funding for Women on Welfare			
Republicans	35	54	11
Democrats (excluding evangelical delegates)	58	30	12
Evangelical Candidate Delegates	1	93	6
Affirmative Action Quotas			
Republicans	6	86	8
Democrats (excluding evangelical delegates)	27	55	19
Evangelical Candidate Delegates	13	70	16

*Source: Abramowitz, et al., 1978b:14-15.

groups, and (4) the unprecedented response from those of evangelical faith who were unschooled and inexperienced in political activism.

Initial indications suggested that evangelicals who participated in the campaign were quite conservative in their stance on issues of life style and morality, more conservative than other Democrats and often more conservative than Republicans (see Table 1).[1] Conservatism in life style has generally been associated with conservative theology and a lack of involvement in political activism among evangelicals. This incongruity between the traditional stance of noninvolvement and the recent activism of seemingly conservative evangeli-

[1]The Virginia Delegate Survey was administered at both the Republican and Democratic Nominating Conventions by Professors Alan Abramowitz, John McGlennon and Ronald Rapoport of the College of William and Mary. Questionnaires were "distributed at the respective

cals prompted this case study. The objective of the research was to ascertain who, by theological conviction and life style characteristics, participated in this political action, how they were motivated, and what was the nature of their goals. This information would lead to an assessment of whether participation in this campaign was an anomaly or a bellwether of change in the orientation of evangelicals to politics.

POLITICAL PARTICIPATION IN A THEORETICAL CONTEXT

Because of the conservatism in belief and life style found among these evangelicals and the social bases of support developed by the candidate, the explanations for this unprecedented movement into politics are set within the framework of the theory of status politics. This approach is in contrast to most theories, which premise economic motivations for political movements. The theory of status politics has evolved from the distinction Weber made between class and status group orientations.

According to Weber, there exist within a community a social order and an economic order, each possessing potential to influence the other. The economic order is defined by the participation of various groups (classes) in the distribution of material resources and the knowledge of their use. In contrast, groups defined by the distribution of prestige characterize the social order. Status is derived from the degree of prestige (termed variously social honor or social esteem) accorded by the community to the group based on some specific shared quality of that group. Such qualities, taken collectively, characterize a particular life style. A similar life style can be expected of all who belong or wish to belong to a group. Closure of the group is thus achieved, and the exclusiveness of membership is dependent on the ability to display the necessary qualifications for membership (Weber, 1946: 187-91).

Though a group may be accorded prestige based on the possession of material resources, this is but one quality which characterizes a group; as such, material wealth need not be present in order for a group to achieve status (Weber, 1946:187). Prestige is accorded to a group in varying positive or negative degrees depending on the perceived worthiness or valuation of the elements which define the group—elements such as "values, beliefs, con-

convention halls to each city and county delegation based on the number of convention votes which the delegation would cast (Abramowitz, et al., 1978b:2-3). No attempt was made to follow up on unreturned questionnaires. Thus the response rate at the Democratic Convention was only 481 of the possible 2,795 delegates (17 percent), and at the Republican Convention, only 455 of the 7,800 delegates (6 percent). Though the biases inherent in this data collection procedure are obvious, the results do give some indication of the stance of the state-wide evangelical contingent.

This table has been amended from a more extensive table presented by Abramowitz, McGlennon, and Rapoport in an unpublished paper, "Summary Results of the Virginia Delegate Survey" (1978b). Percentages are based on the numbers of respondents indicated above.

sumption habits, and the cultural items differentiating nonclass groups from each other'' (Gusfield, 1963:18). A hierarchical arrangement of groups is based on the amount of prestige received. Placement in the hierarchy of status groups (like that of social classes) determines how members of a specific group will approach and be approached in social interaction, thus reflecting the relative power of the group.

In both the economic and the social order, power is defined as the probability of given individuals or groups ''to realize their own will in a communal action even against the resistance of others who are participating in the action'' (Weber, 1946:180). Thus, power may be exerted by a group—either a class or a status group—to influence the distribution of material resources or the distribution of prestige, respectively.

Using Weber's definition of status and status group orientations, Richard Hofstadter and Seymour Martin Lipset were early contributors (during the 1950s) to the development of the theory of status politics in their explanations of support for the Progressive Movement, the Ku Klux Klan, and McCarthyism. Each of these groups was seen as attempting to affect the distribution of prestige, and thus of power. In 1963, Gusfield further developed this explanation of political conflict in his treatment of the American Temperance Movement in the volume, *Symbolic Crusade*. In his work, Gusfield pointed out the symbolic nature of specific conflicts aimed at restoring, maintaining, or enhancing the prestige of a particular life style.

More recent works, such as those of Zurcher, et al. (1971) and Page and Clelland (1978), have amended the theory still further to explain political struggles over moral principles and the protection of life style. Respectively, these analyses dealt with a controversy over acceptable textbooks and a conflict over distribution of pornographic materials.

Change in perspective is apparent in the contemporary use of the theory of status politics. Emphasis is now placed on life style protection rather than on status enhancement. Because particular life styles are accorded varying degrees of prestige and the relative amount of prestige received determines a given group's status, it is apparent that status is indeed defined by society's valuation of a particular life style. Thus, Page and Clelland do not see status politics as ''the attempt to defend against declining prestige but the attempt to defend a way of life'' (Page and Clelland, 1978:266). They state, ''style of life can be maintained or propagated only to the extent that its adherents exercise some control over the means of socialization and social intercourse'' (Page and Clelland, 1978:267). This attempt to defend a way of life is readily apparent in the motivations of Progressives, Ku Klux Klanners, McCarthyites, Prohibitionists, and opponents of pornography.

The issues around which such groups rally in an attempt to protect a life style are often symbolic; that is, they are relatively narrow in scope but stand for a larger whole. This is not out of keeping with political conflicts in the economic sphere. Control of the influences that bear upon the maintenance of a life style is essential, yet an issue relatively narrow in scope may stand for and serve to reinforce a way of life—a system of belief. Conflicts come as a result of attempts by opposing groups "to build and sustain moral orders which provide basic meaning for human lives" (Page and Clelland, 1978:279). "Protestors are expressing a direct concern about the erosion of their control over their way of life" (265). Page and Clelland, thus, have replaced the term "status politics" with "the politics of life style concerns," a term more aptly descriptive of the expressed motivations for such movements (Page and Clelland, 1978:266-67).

Clarification of the concepts—status, prestige, and life style[2]—and their use in this context leads to an ease of application and a better understanding of non-economic political movements. In those earlier analyses that focused on status discontent as the motivating factor of such movements, it was necessary to document a perception of and threat to the status of a group as well as a motivation to enhance or preserve that status. In later analyses of such movements, focus on life style rather than on status facilitated the identification of motivations in empirical analyses. Participants in what have been called status movements perceive and verbalize their actions as a means of protecting their life style rather than their status. A primary concern with the preservation of life style is apparent in all the descriptions of non-economic political movements.

That a dominant life style is accorded greater prestige, and thus higher status, cannot be denied. That placement in the status hierarchy also influences the power of a given group is apparent. However, in the social realm, life style is the exogenous variable with prestige, status, and power dependent thereupon. To focus on status is theoretically to put the cart before the horse and expect locomotion.

Thus, life style concern is the *motivating factor,* and preservation and protection of a life style are the *goals* of non-economic political movements. As such, these goals are instrumental in nature. The *tactics* employed to reach the goal of life style protection may be either *instrumental,* oriented directly at protecting or defending a life style, or *symbolic,* representing the many

[2] These concepts are well-defined by Zurcher, et al., 1971: "'Social status' refers to the distribution of prestige among individuals and groups in a social system. 'Prestige' means the approval, respect, admiration, or deference a person or group is able to command by virtue of his or its imputed qualities of performances. 'Style of life' refers to the system of values, customs, and habits distinctive to a . . . group."

instances and circumstances that call for action but are not directly connected to the goal.

The subject of the present research is a conservative group, previously inactive in politics, which recently entered the political arená. It was hypothesized that the motivation for such action was concern over the preservation of a life style and, further, that the goal of this action was life style protection. In this instance, merely to place a representative in political office is to employ a tactic which symbolically legitimates a way of life. Conversely, to expect such a representative purposely to effect legislation is to employ an instrumental tactic to bring about accomplishment of the goal—life style protection.

SAMPLING PROCEDURE AND DESCRIPTION OF RESPONDENTS

Interviews were conducted with supporters of the evangelical candidate who attended two local mass meetings—one in a city and one in a county district in Virginia. One hundred and thirty-six registered voters who attended these meetings declared their support for the evangelical candidate; subsequently 13 were elected as delegates to the State Nominating Convention. In-depth, personal interviews with 12 of these 13 delegates yielded the qualitative data that is the basis of this research. In addition, telephone interviews were solicited with a 50 percent random sample (N=62) of individuals selected from among the remaining mass meeting attendees who declared their support for the evangelical candidate. Among these persons, 55 interviews were completed, an 89 percent response rate. These telephone interviews provided the quantitative data in support of the qualitative findings. For ease in future reporting, these two samples will be referred to as the "delegate sample" and the "mass sample." Significant differences between samples are explained to allow a qualitative analysis supported by the findings from the quantitative sample.

In age, education, income, socioeconomic status,[3] marital status and number of children per family, no significant difference between the delegate and mass samples was found. There was, however, a significant difference in sex between the two samples. Ninety-two percent of the delegate sample was male, 8 percent female (N=12); 49 percent of the mass sample was male, 51 percent female (N=55). The predominance of males as delegates supports the traditional view of the male leadership role which would be expected among conservative evangelicals (Quebedeaux, 1978:77-8).

[3] A socioeconomic status score was computed using the Duncan Socioeconomic Status Index (SEI) (Featherman, et al., 1975) based on Bureau of Census occupational codes. A family SEI score was computed using the respondent's SEI score if unmarried, the husband's score when married, and the wife's score when married with the husband unemployed. The possible range of these scores was 3 to 96.

TABLE 2

SAMPLE DIFFERENCES

	Delegate Sample			Mass Sample			Difference	
	Mean	s.d.	N	Mean	s.d.	N		
Age	34.6 yrs.	10.79	12	34.1 yrs	11.22	55	t=.14,	p=.89
Education	16.5 yrs.	3.00	12	15.3 yrs.	2.72	53	t=1.33,	p=.23
Income	$20,333	162.56	12	$15,424	99.08	53	t=1.0,	p=.33
Socioeconomic Status	59	17.25	12	49	27.92	54	t=1.2,	p=.12
Children per Family	1.6	1.51	10	2.0	1.98	44	t=.67,	p=.49
Length of Neighborhood Residence	1.6 yrs.	1.58	12	4.2 yrs.	4.18	55	t=−2.38,	p=<.01
	% of Respondents			% of Respondents				
Sex	92% male 8% female N=12			49% male 51% female N=55 X^2=5.64, df=1, p=.02				
Marital Status	83% married 17% unmarried N=12			70% married 30% unmarried N=55 X^2=1.63, df=4, p=.80				

One further difference in life style was found significant: the length of residence in one's neighborhood (see Table 2). Though the indication is that delegates were a more geographically mobile group, this has little bearing on this research. With these two exceptions—sex and length of residence—no differences between the samples on demographic or life style characteristics were found.

No significant difference in theological belief was found between the delegate sample and the mass sample; however, those in the delegate sample were more inclined to witness their faith for the purpose of converting others than were those in the mass sample. The leadership role in which delegates were cast is likely associated with the ability to influence others. This may explain the difference found.

A significant difference was found between the samples on an index of political knowledge. Individuals in the delegate sample tended to be more knowledgeable of those in political office; however, the experience of having been a delegate may have influenced this.

One further difference was found between the samples: they varied in reasons for attending the mass meeting. This difference is related to the process by which individuals became delegates. Those in the delegate sample were more likely to have had personal contact with the candidate, and this was their reason for attending the mass meeting.

LIFE STYLE ORIENTATION

The common denominator among those who participated in the subject political action was their adherence to an evangelical faith—that is, they believe in the full authority of the Scriptures, the necessity of a conversion experience as a means to salvation, and the necessity of evangelism. This belief system provides for evangelicals an organization of life. In relating their experience before coming to evangelicalism, respondents described a search for spirituality and an ethical orientation to life which was fulfilled upon conversion to this faith. *Rebirth is a reorientation to life* guided by faith, as well as a means to salvation.

Unity among this group outweighed a diversity of affiliation and evangelical orientation. While some belonged to evangelical factions within denominational churches—Baptist, Episcopal, Mennonite, and Presbyterian—the vast majority, 82 percent (N =55), belonged to nondenominational bodies. Within the nondenominational bodies were charismatics as well as conservative evangelicals. The diversity in affiliation and orientation was not met with a well-defined separation of identity among these evangelicals. All those of an evangelical faith are identified as "believers." Friendships cut across denominational and nondenominational affiliations, and ties of association are maintained through religiously-oriented social contacts. These ties and a common evangelical faith contributed to a collective identity which superceded variation in affiliation and orientation and thus provided a common base for concerted political action.

Those from denominational groups accounted for the few instances of more liberal theological interpretation. Those from the nondenominational groups were conservative as indicated by a literal interpretation of the Bible and a creationist view of the origins of man. Given that the majority of these individuals were of a nondenominational affiliation, a conservative theological interpretation was most pervasive.

Conservatism in theological belief was accompanied, as expected, by an individualistic approach to social problems: 85 percent (N =55) of the respondents emphasized evangelism aimed at individual regeneration as a solution to social ills. This approach to social concern does not explain the movement into political action. However, since conversion to the evangelical faith brings a reorientation to life in the present, a conservative life style based on theological belief is affirmed. It becomes important to these individuals to maintain and protect their life style. The possibility to "live well as far as faith is concerned" provides a key to explaining political action on the part of theologically conservative evangelicals.

Solidarity and commitment to the evangelical faith and life style were maintained through the structure and frequency of social interaction among members of these evangelical groups. All respondents reported attending church services weekly, and in 35 percent (N=55) of the cases, two to three times a week. Sixty-one percent (N=55) of the respondents reported also meeting in smaller groups for Bible study and prayer meetings. One respondent aptly described how these smaller groups strengthen commitment. He stated that interaction

has to be in small groups because if you belong to anything big, ... a lot is lost ... .But in the smaller group—seven, eight, or ten people that meet all the time—it's a family. When someone is hurting, you can't deny that you know it. There's a commitment here to one another. This is the family structure, not the biological family, but a family ... and the responsibilities of the family are there. Then, of course, we share to the larger family—[the congregation]. But if you don't belong to a very small family, you have no commitment.

The analogy to the family and the dependence and acceptance found therein was used frequently by evangelicals in describing the individuals and groups to which they are committed.

Sixty-five percent of the respondents also reported attending such religiously-oriented social groups as Christian Women's Club, Women Aglow, and Full Gospel Business Men's Fellowship. Eighty-three percent (N=55) reported that half or more of their social activities were church-related. A moderately high association (r_s=.37, p=.01, N=53) was found between the degree to which social activities were church-related and close friends were of the same faith—further evidence that such interaction enhanced the development of a close-knit group of persons of similar social and religious orientation.

The impact of social change in the secular culture of America was also an influence on these evangelicals and, in many instances, was a cause for deep concern. Such concern centered especially on the pervasiveness of liberal influences that come to bear on the family.

The ideal family was seen as a close-knit unit in which husband and wife assume traditional roles. As one respondent explained the basis of this relationship:

God has set up a God-ordained authority structure where God is the head of Christ, Christ is the head of man, and man is the head of woman .... The man is ordained by God to be the head of the home, of the household, of the family unit; and this is the system that works best for human society.

Variation in the interpretation of this "ideal" authority structure existed. However, the influence of this traditional model based on theological principles was apparent regardless of interpretation. Also, conservatism concerning the female role was more readily apparent within this group than it is among the population as a whole. Respondents were asked four questions from a national survey concerning the changing role of women (Anonymous, 1979). Though 53 percent (N=35) of these couples included an employed wife, these evangelicals were more likely than the population as a whole to see a wife's primary role as that of mother and homemaker. They were also more apt than the general population to perceive deleterious effects to children when the mother is employed. Though a move away from the traditional roles of wife as homemaker and husband as breadwinner may be seen even within this conservative group, such a trend is problematic to a group trying to maintain a traditional family structure based on scriptural principles.

Apprehension and even outrage were expressed at the influences that bear upon children. The family is not only a protective environment in which to rear children, but it is also the stage for socialization to the evangelical faith. Secular influences, at times, were seen as contrary to this process, especially those influences that are institutionalized in the public schools. As related by a respondent, this concern centered around

prohibiting the name of God to be mentioned in schools, prayers and Bible reading out of the schools, ... requiring secular humanism to be taught in schools—that man is able to meet all his own needs, [is] self-sufficient. It exalts the man!

These evangelicals exhibited only a moderate affirmation of such secular activities as dancing, consumption of alcohol, and use of tobacco. They opposed gambling and the use of marijuana and were adamant in their stand against abortion. Indignation was expressed over the perceived implications and possible effects on the family of the Equal Rights Amendment.

The life style of these evangelicals was centered on church and family and was seen as different from that of others. This difference, however, was seen as a key to the betterment of self and society. As one respondent related:

believers are going to have different behaviors—they are going to be different. I think that an example that the Lord used that we are the salt of the earth is certainly appropriate. I think as we live the believing life that we're going to have an influence on the country, as a preservative in terms of the moral climate and also as a flavoring in terms of just making the country still acceptable in terms of the Lord's sights.

The necessity of preserving the moral climate of America is, in effect, a means of preserving a life style, the evangelical life style. Much in the secular culture of America is at odds with the evangelical stance, especially the moral atmosphere and philosophies upon which it is based. In addition, many sociopolitical issues under consideration and many legislative actions were seen as symbolically supporting a more liberal life style. One respondent stated:

I feel as if the country is drifting away from the principles and stances that have in the past made it a strong country. I think that the Senate, especially the Senate, has gotten very liberal in their leanings and their philosophy.

This view was echoed by another:

there's a whole attitude in the country now that there is no right and wrong, that if it feels good, ... then that's up to you. There's a breakdown of some sort of an ethic, and it's becoming a situation ethic type of thing. I think there needs to be a very strong Christian stance toward that type of attitude that I feel is pervading.

And yet a third respondent stated:

In evangelical Christianity, there is a strong, strong concern ... for the state of the nation.

It is with this background that evangelical Christians approached the political arena in support of a candidate of like orientation.

MOVEMENT INTO POLITICAL ACTIVISM

The participants who actively supported the evangelical candidate were Republicans, Democrats, and independent voters, although a Republican influence was most pervasive. Forty-five percent (N=49) identified themselves as Republicans or reported a tendency to vote Republican. Twenty-nine percent reported Democratic orientations, and 26 percent identified themselves as completely independent. As one respondent explained:

basically [evangelical] Christians are conservative in terms of their political belief and would normally tend to favor a Republican candidate who would be labeled conservative.

This observation was further supported by self-identification: 38 percent (N=52) identified themselves as conservative, 31 percent as middle-of-the-road, and only 10 percent felt they were liberal or radical in their political orientations. The remaining 21 percent of the respondents stated they did not know how to classify themselves.

Delegates from across the state who supported the evangelical candidate displayed a similar pattern of conservatism in political orientation, especially on morally-laden political issues. They were often more conservative even than Republicans. Yet the evangelical candidate's supporters aligned themselves with the Democratic party though many had tended toward a Republican orientation on issues and in previous partisan identification. This suggests that their motive was more the means by which they might put an evangelical in office than their agreement with the stance of the party under whose banner their candidate ran.

These evangelicals had very little prior experience in active support of a political candidate. Furthermore, only 45 percent (N=55) reported "usually"[4] voting in national, state, and local elections during the past three years, as compared to 70 percent (N=2549) in a national sample (Verba and Nie, 1972). An anomaly in the evangelical group's pattern of low political participation is that 36 percent of this group reported contacting elected representatives about problems or issues of concern; this is almost three times the rate found in the national sample. The evangelicals' contacts related to morally-laden issues such as abortion, curricula and prayer in schools, and the Equal Rights Amendment. This, indeed, is an indication of concern that existed prior to the present political action and, in part, explains the ease with which this group was mobilized.

As indicated, this group of evangelicals exhibited conservatism in theological and social orientations. They saw themselves as apart from the mainstream of secular culture and exhibited considerable solidarity within their group. Concern was expressed over decline in moral standards and the consequent influences that bear on the evangelical life style. Though numerous attempts had been made to influence the stand of elected representative, these evangelicals had not been active in support of candidates for elected office.

This background of conservatism, concern, and noninvolvement was utilized in gaining their support. The candidate whom they supported not only possessed a faith and social orientation similar to theirs but also presented himself as a political novice with a calling to duty. He identified evangelicals' lack of involvement in politics as the reason they are unable to control the influences that are a source of their concern. He also educated them in the political process by which they might make their voices heard.

This appeal for active involvement was combined with a system of outreach to the evangelical community that utilized the existing structure of evangelical

[4]That is, they voted 75 percent or more of the time, missing no more than one voting opportunity in the past three years.

social contacts. Given that this is a close-knit group of similar orientation, few initial contacts were necessary to develop a considerable basis of support in a short period of time. The effectiveness of using this social network to develop support can be seen in that 84 percent (N=55) of supporters at the mass meetings learned of the candidate through church and friends. Cassette tapes announcing the candidacy and the political process necessary for support were sent to church groups; however, these tapes and conventional media sources had much less effect.

This candidate's appeal for involvement was received by evangelicals trying to maintain a traditional, morally conservative life style—who express concern over governmental actions that legitimate and, through their symbolic connotation, give greater prestige to a more liberal element of American society. In a "symbolic crusade" aimed at preserving the life style to which they are committed, the tactic of these evangelicals was to place a representative of like orientation in a position of political prestige and power in order that he might bring recognition to their values. Fifty-nine percent (N=55) of those who supported this evangelical candidate hoped only that he would bring a "Christian influence" to bear; 27 percent anticipated that he might bring "integrity" and "a moral influence" to government. Only 10 percent voiced a desire for legislative action, and 4 percent for responsible government. In the possibility to bring a morally conservative "Christian influence" to government is the possibility to legitimate and protect the conservative evangelical life style.

Though the candidate did not win the nomination, the success of the movement was apparent to those who participated. In a short period of time evangelicals had rallied and effectively made an impact on the political sphere. And, while only 9 percent (N=55) had ever participated in such an action previously, 71 percent (N=55) stated they will again work for the election of a political representative. Their efforts now are aimed at educating evangelicals state-wide on how to continue involvement. The basis of political activism has been laid; a course of future participation appears probable. Thus, the success of this movement appears to be not an anomaly but a precursor to continued political involvement by evangelicals.

CONCLUSION

The 1978 race for a U.S. Senator from Virginia saw the onset of political activism among previously uninvolved, conservative evangelical Christians. The seeds of activism were sown during the past decades as the divergence in social orientation between this traditionally oriented group and the more liberal secular culture became more apparent. A perceived decline in morals and the perception of legislative issues that symbolically support a more liberal element of American society have motivated evangelicals of various orientations—non-denominational as well as denominational, conservative as well as charismatic—to this concerted political activism. In a symbolic crusade aimed at preserving the life style to which they are committed, the tactic of these evangelicals was to place a representative of like orientation in a position of political prestige and power in order that he might bring a "Christian influence" and "high moral standards" to bear. In this was seen the possibility to preserve the moral climate of America and, in so doing, legitimate and protect the conservative evangelical life style.

REFERENCES

Abramowitz, Alan, John McGlennon, and Ronald Rapoport. 1978a. "The 1978 Virginia senatorial nominating conventions." *The University of Virginia, Institute of Government News Letter*, 55 (December):13-6.

1978b. Summary results of Virginia delegate survey. Unpublished Paper.

Anonymous. 1979. "Opinion roundup—the modern woman: how far has she come?" *Public Opinion*, (January/February):35-40.

Brandmeyer, G. A., and R. S. Denisoff. 1969. "Status politics: an appraisal of the application of a concept." *Pacific Sociological Review*, 12:5-11.

Featherman, David L., Michael Sabel and David Dickens. 1975. A manual for coding occupations and industries into detailed 1970 categories and a listing of 1970 basic Duncan socioeconomic and NORC prestige scores, working paper #75-1. Unpublished Paper. University of Wisconsin.

Gerstner, John M. 1975. "The theological boundaries of evangelical faith." Pp. 21-37 in David F. Wells and John D. Woodbridge (eds.), *The Evangelicals*. Nashville, Tenn.: Abingdon Press.

Gusfield, Joseph R. 1963. Symbolic Crusade: Status Politics and the American Temperance Movement. Urbana: University of Illinois Press.

Hofstadter, Richard. 1955. The Age of Reform: From Bryan to F.D.R. Garden City, New York: Doubleday.

1963. "The pseudo-conservative revolt (1955)." Pp. 75-95 in Daniel Bell (ed.), *The Radical Right: The New American Right Expanded and Updated*. Garden City, New York: Doubleday.

1963. "Pseudo-conservative revolt revisited: a postscript (1962)." Pp. 97-103 in Daniel Bell (ed.), *The Radical Right: The New American Right Expanded and Updated*. Garden City, New York: Doubleday.

Linder, Robert D. 1975. "The resurgence of evangelical social concern (1925-75)." Pp. 189-210 in David F. Wells and John D. Woodbridge (eds.), *The Evangelicals*. Nashville, Tenn.: Abingdon Press.

Lipset, Seymour Martin. 1955. "The sources of the 'radical right.'" Pp. 166-233 in Daniel Bell (ed.), *The New American Right*. New York: Criterion Books.

Marsden, George M. 1975. "From fundamentalism to evangelicalism: a historical analysis." Pp. 122-42 in David F. Wells and John Woodbridge (eds.), *The Evangelicals*. Nashville, Tenn.: Abingdon Press.

Moberg, David O. 1972. The Great Reversal: Evangelism Versus Social Concern. Philadelphia: J. B. Lippincott Co.

Page, Ann L. and Donald A. Clelland. 1978. "The Kanawha County textbook controversy: a study of the politics of life style concern." *Social Forces*, 57:265-81.

Pierard, Richard B. 1970. The Unequal Yoke: Evangelical Christianity and Political Conservatism. Philadelphia: Lippincott.

Quebedeaux, Richard. 1978. The Worldly Evangelicals. New York: Harper & Row.

Verba, Sidney and Norman H. Nie. 1972. Participation in America: Political Democracy and Social Equality. New York: Harper & Row.

Weber, Max. 1946. From Max Weber: Essays in Sociology. (eds. and trans.) H. H. Gerth and C. Wright Mills. New York: Oxford.

Zurcher, Louis A., Jr., *et al.* 1971. "The anti-pornography campaign: a symbolic crusade." *Social Problems*, 19:217-38.

7

TELEVANGELISM AND THE NEW CHRISTIAN RIGHT

Jeffrey K. Hadden

After attending a Moral Majority meeting in the fall of 1980, one of the participants came away with the following remark:

Falwell stated that they were meeting on a political—not a religious—platform, but then they prayed. He stated again that it was not a religious meeting, but then they read the Scripture. Again, he reiterated that it was not a religious meeting, but then he preached for 40 minutes (Bumpas, 1980:5).

Then the commentator went on to conclude that "An organization that is started by a preacher and is led by preachers who conduct themselves like preachers is a religious organization" (Bumpas, 1980:5).

There is great confusion, even anguish, in America today about the relationship between religion and politics. Thomas Jefferson thought he could distinguish between the expression of religious opinion and seditious preaching. In his mind, the former was protected by the First Amendment, the latter was not. Many liberals, disturbed by the emergence of the New Christian Right, would like to erect the firm wall of separation between church and state of which Mr. Jefferson wrote in his celebrated letter of 1802 to the Danbury, Connecticut, Baptist Association.

Jefferson's vision of an ideal relationship between church and state, notwithstanding, there never has been much of a wall separating religion and politics. One can even argue that the two are naturally inseparable in modern pluralistic cultures. Secular ideals of justice and good are firmly anchored in ideals of religious morality. As Randall Collins has noted, "the sermon is the antecedent of the political speech" (Collins, 1975: 377).

Virtually all social movements borrow the symbols of religious identification to legitimize their causes, whether or not they are religious. Why,

Portions of this paper were abstracted from *Prime Time Preachers* (co-authored with Charles E. Swann) Addison-Wesley Publishers, 1981.

therefore, shouldn't a Baptist preacher on a political stump bring along his repertoire of religious symbols? (I'm not certain whether Jerry Falwell self-consciously blurs the roles of politician and preacher, or if he is just so thoroughly a preacher that when he steps into a different role his master role cannot be masked. I have a hunch that it is the latter.)

What troubles a lot of Americans today is not the mixing of religion and politics. Rather, the problem is that they don't like the politics of the fundamentalists. And, many have worried themselves into a state of hysteria about the implications of fundamentalists becoming as zealous about their politcs as they are about their faith.

Today many Paul Reveres and Jack Jouetts sound the cry that the fascists are coming. No useful purpose is served by this rhetoric and, in my view, a good many deliterious consequences could follow. The television preachers, who are the vanguard of the New Christian Right, are amassing an enormous power base. The potential for abuse is all too evident. The potential for constructive contributions to American society is almost being totally ignored.

The television preachers and their style of mixing religion and politics is going to be with us for a long while. If their presence on the political scene is disheartening to liberals and moderates, it is all the more important that they begin to understand (a) who these people are, (b) why they have entered the political arena and (c) what kinds of resources they bring.

To launch the task of understanding the New Christian Right, let me quote two brief passages which pack a lot of wisdom. The first comes from Jeremy Rifkin's provocative book, *The Emerging Order:*

Of one thing there is little doubt, the evangelical community is amassing a base of potential power that dwarfs every other competing interest in American society today. A close look at the evangelical communications network ... should convince even the skeptic that it is now the single most important cultural force in American life (Rifkin, 1979:105).

The second text comes from the first chapter of Ben Armstrong's book, *The Electric Church*. Armstrong is the Executive Director of the National Religious Broadcasters.

The electric church has launched a revolution as dramatic as the revolution that began when Martin Luther nailed his ninety-five theses to the cathedral door at Wittenberg. Just as the Reformation brought sweeping changes in the way Christians understood their relationship to God and the way they expressed their devotion through worship, so has the electric church (Armstrong, 1979:10-11).

Twentieth-century technology has truly revolutionized the opportunities to fulfill Christ's great commission to "Go ye into all the world and preach the gospel to every creature'' (Mark 16:15). Even some of the lesser lights of the electronic church are reaching larger audiences than Christ himself reached in a lifetime.

The reasons the electronic church is important—the reason it has captured the concern of America—is told not in audience size or budgets or air time. It is found in the potential clout of these people to reshape American culture. Unlike the smorgasbord of religious pluralism that one can find in virtually every American community, the menu of spiritual messages on the airwaves are substantially limited to fundamentalist and evangelical offerings. While it would be naive and foolish to fail to see the diversity within the fundamentalist and evangelical camps, there is considerable homogeneity in the conservative theological emphasis. And, as repeated social science investigations have demonstrated, there are clear linkages between conservative theology and conservative political ideology. Only a few radio and television preachers have publically pronounced the wedding of conservative theology and conservative politics. The latent linkage, however, is present in almost all of the conservative traditions.

From a long tradition of circuit riders, tent preachers, and Elmer Gantry-like revivalists, the evangelists—now the televangelists—have come a long way. No longer are they simply safeguarding the moral and spiritual character of their private constituency. No longer are they satisfied with Sister Lou or Brother Jim finding the Lord and being born again. For while salvation may still be their goal, the sinner is not you and me any more ... it's America. And to save America takes a lot of believers, a lot of money and a lot of power.

The power of the televangelists lies in their potential to mobilize large masses of everyday Christians. Unlike any other sector of television, the religious broadcasters represent a nascent social movement. Astutely mobilized, their power will not be easily checked. What happened in 1980 as a few television preachers moved boldly into the political arena is that they demonstrated to America that their potential is already real.

Pollster George Gallup declared 1976 the ''Year of the Evangelical.'' It was really the year the press discovered evangelicals. They exist in huge numbers—30 to 85 million depending on the criteria employed to define evangelicals. Jimmy Carter's public profession that he was a ''born again'' Christian had much to do with our discovery of evangelicals. And when the votes were counted and the analysts had finished their analyzing of voting patterns, it seemed reasonably clear that Jimmy Carter's margin of victory on his improbable march to the White House may well have been provided by evangelicals.

Most analysts, however, either missed or underplayed the importance of this group as a potentially powerful voting block in future elections. There was a tendency to see Carter's candidacy and victory as an aberration in American political history. He ran primarily *against Washington* in the fallout of Watergate. His opponent was an accidental president who was prone to accidents. Television cameras frequently caught President Gerald Ford stumbling down steps and bumping his head on helicopter doors, and when he played golf he sometimes bumped other people's heads. And no one could ever forget those immortal words, attributed to Lyndon Johnson, about Jerry Ford being too dumb to walk and chew gum at the same time. In many people's minds, Jimmy Carter was also a kind of accidental president. Thus, there was no real need to seriously assess the significance of the "evangelical vote."

George Gallup didn't get a chance to declare 1980 the "Year of Born-Again Politics." The evangelicals beat him to it.

In late 1979 a number of television preachers began meeting quietly with the prospective presidential candidates. There were perhaps a dozen meetings in all with various members of the electronic church in attendance. As the primaries began and the list of presidential hopefuls shrank, so also did the list of television preachers willing to go out on the limb and declare a political agenda. Most who were initially involved fell back to the position that it is a Christian's duty to be an informed and involved citizen. Even this, however, is an important move toward the politicization of elements of the evangelical and fundamentalist communities. Many have long taken an other-worldly view, shunning the political affairs of this world, including the exercise of voting rights.

The first apparent evidence of political thunder from evangelical Christians occurred in late April when about a quarter-of-a-million of them came to Washington for two days of prayer and repentance. Pat Robertson, head of Christian Broadcasting Network, and Bill Bright, founder of Campus Crusade for Christ, co-chaired the *Washington for Jesus* program. Here's Bright on the Washington Mall:

If you want to trace something, read Deuteronomy, Chapters 8 and 28, and Amos, Chapter 4. It will give you an idea of why we are going through the persecution, the chastening, the judgment of God that we are experiencing today. It's no mystery. We've turned from God and God is chastening us. Laugh if you will. The critics will laugh. And they'll make fun. But I'll tell you, this is God's doing. You go back to 1962 and 3 and you'll discover a series of plagues came upon America. First, the assassination of President Kennedy; the war in Viet Nam accelerated; the drug culture swept millions of our young people into this drug scene; the youth revolution, crime accelerated over 300 percent in a brief period of time; the racial conflict threatened to tear our nation apart, and the Watergate scandal. The divorce rate accelerated and there were almost as many divorces as marriages. And there was an epidemic of teenage pregnancies, an epidemic of venereal disease; an epidemic of drug addiction; an epidemic of alcoholism. And now, we are faced with a great economic crisis ... God is saying to us, Wake Up! Wake Up! Wake Up! (Bright, addressing *Washington for Jesus* Rally, Washington, D.C., April, 1980).

Bright and Robertson spent a lot of time trying to persuade a skeptical press corps that the event was nonpolitical. Several factors made it difficult for these otherwise effective communicators to be persuasive. There was a highly partisan document called "A Christian Declaration" which was withdrawn before it became an official statement of purpose, but not before it had been rather widely circulated. There was also an embarrassing letter sent to all Senators and Representatives from a person identifying himself as a congressional liaison for *Washington for Jesus*. And they had organized the entire gathering by congressional districts so that people could better be prepared to call on their elected representatives in government. Disclaimers of political intent notwithstanding, there was sufficient appearance of politics to result in a ranking U.S. Senator threatening to investigate the tax exempt status of the ministeries of the organization's leadership.

Media consciousness of the involvement of conservative Christians in politics increased several fold when Jerry Falwell and his Moral Majority showed up in force at the National Republican Convention in Detroit. When the electronic preachers assembled a few weeks later in Dallas for a National Affairs Briefing, the media showed up in force—more than 250 strong. An additional hundred or so members of the press corps showed up with Ronald Reagan when he addressed a screaming crowd of 15,000 on 22 August. Departing from his prepared text, Reagan began by saying:

A few days ago I addressed a group in Chicago and received their endorsement for my candidacy. Now I know this is a nonpartisan gathering and so I know you can't endorse me, but I only brought that up because I want you to know that I endorse you and what you are doing (Reagan, addressing National Affairs Briefing in Dallas, August 1980).

Within a matter of days, there was hardly anyone in the media, print or broadcast, who didn't know that there was a New Christian Right and that they were moving into the political arena in force. And the media proceeded to inform America. The press zeroed in on Falwell and the Moral Majority. He appeared on the cover of *Newsweek* and quickly became one of the most sought after figures in the 1980 campaign. His many guest appearances included *Meet the Press, Today* and the *Phil Donahue Show*. He also addressed the National Press Club. When he wasn't present, he was often the subject of conversation, much of it rather derogatory.

Christian leaders, both liberal and conservative, took the initiative in speaking out against the born-again politicians. Individual criticism soon became an avalanche of organized attack as large segments of the liberal press and secular organizations jumped on the band wagon to denounce the New Christian Right. When leaders were unable to mobilize official resolutions on behalf of their organizations, they joined with other leaders from similiar organizations to release joint communications. For example, leaders of fifteen major Protestant denominations released a statement which they called "Christian Theological Observations on the Religious Right Movement."

In addition to the mobilization of existing organizations denouncing the New Christian Right, new organizations sprang up for that purpose. Norman Lear, creator of *All in the Family* and a lion's share of other successful television sitcoms of the 1970s, hastily assembled a blue ribbon board of some of America's more prominent liberals in religion, education, publishing and entertainment and created an organization called People for the American Way. Created for the purpose of promoting religious pluralism, the first visible effort of PAW was a series of television spots that went after the televangelists.

By the time the 1980 elections rolled around, the corralling of 1600 Pennsylvania by a one-time cowboy movie actor wasn't totally unexpected. Long associated with the right wing of the Republican Party, Ronald Reagan was not considered sufficiently scary to offset the liabilities the Carter Administration had amassed. What was not expected on that second Tuesday of November, however, was the virtual annihilation of the liberal leadership of the Congress that was running for reelection. Millions of liberal American's felt their hearts drop to the pits of their stomachs as they watched the election returns. One by one, the liberal Senators went down to defeat: Frank Church, Birch Bayh, John Culver, George McGovern, Warren Magnuson and Gaylord Nelson—all replaced by persons of much more conservative persuasion.

By the election Jerry Falwell and the Moral Majority had practically become household words. Falwell wasted no time in stepping forward to claim responsibility in the name of Moral Majority and fellow New Christian Right organizations. Pollster Louis Harris agreed with this assessment. So did a number of the Senators and Congressmen who had gone down in defeat.

The shock of the election results, plus the attribution of the outcome to Christian zealots, set in motion a chain reaction of fear that has not been experienced in America since the early 1950s when Senator Joseph McCarthy terrorized everyone who disagreed with his views. The American Civil Liberties Union sent an urgent appeal to its membership to fight and ran a full-page advertisement in the Sunday New York Times with a banner which read: "IF THE MORAL MAJORITY HAS ITS WAY, YOU'D BETTER START PRAYING." Everywhere there was a sense that America was being overrun, not by sensible garden-variety conservatives like Bill Buckley and George Will, but by crazies hell bent on shoving their brand of Americanism and Christianity down the throats of the rest of society.

Is this fear an overreaction? Would the acquisition of real political power by these born-again policiticians result in a massive assault on First Amendment rights? Would liberal values of all sorts be suppressed? Where would they stop? Where would they draw the line on the imposition of their values and life style on the rest of society? Are they really out to establish a theocracy? Would they create a society like unto the Iranian state in the hands of religious madmen?

Jerry Falwell says the press and the liberal establishment has overreacted and not really heard what he is saying. He claims Moral Majority doesn't want to Christianize the nation. They just want their chance—like everybody else—to get in their say. He says he believes in religious and cultural pluralism and has no intentions of walking on the First Amendment rights of anyone. And privately he will admit that in his enthusiasm he sometimes overstates his point of view.

Who are these people, the New Christian Right? Why their seemingly sudden move into politics? What are their goals? What strategies do they employ? What resources do they command?

The New Christian Right is a coalescence of a range of diverse and previously only loosely connected groups. Many are single-issue groups, such as anti-abortion and anti-ERA organizations. The hallways of the Reunion Arena in Dallas were crowded with exhibits and the literature of two dozen exhibitors including Christian Voice, Pro Family Forum, National Prayer Campaign, Eagle Forum, Right to Life Commission, Fund to Restore an Educated Electorate and the Institute for Christian Economics. And there were several newspapers like *Christian Inquirer* and *Christian Courier* which have sought to be catalysts to bring together the diverse causes and interests represented in these groups.

While they have diverse interests and goals, they share in common an anger about what is happening to America which is grounded in their evangelical faith. American culture has moved significantly in directions that seriously affront their personal beliefs. Explicit sex in print and broadcast media are morally wrong, they feel, and there is a clear causal relationship between this development and the soaring divorce rate, living together out of wedlock, casual sex, etc. Abortion is the taking of human life. Talk of the rights of women to determine whether to carry a pregnancy, is to use language to hide the truth that millions of unborn babies have been murdered.

But these issues represent only the tip of the iceberg. Their anger and moral indignation runs deep, and their resentment about what is happening in and to America has been growing for a long time. Perhaps what angers them most is the fact that they don't believe the rest of society and the government, in particular, has taken them seriously. They are tired of being treated as a lunatic fringe or just another interest group that isn't strong enough to be factored into political decisions. Partly because their own values have held politics to be dirty, and partly because the political process has discounted their importance, they have developed feelings of powerlessness and second-class citizenship.

From their vantage point, this nation has fallen from greatness because it has turned its back on God. Getting right with God requires repentance and cleaning up a lot of individual and collective sin. Substantial segments of this belief system have been shared by evangelicals for many years. Billy Graham's crusades haven't strayed very far from these themes in a quarter-of-a-century.

The new ingredient in this emerging coalition is the belief that it is the *responsibility*, indeed the *duty*, of Christians to engage in the political process as a means of bringing America back to God. And like the liberals of the 1950 and 60s, they believe morality can be legislated. Hence, it is important to get the right people elected to office. Congressman Guy Vander Jagt, who electrified the National Republican Convention with his keynote address, accomplished no less when he told the National Affairs Briefing that it is a Christian's duty to get involved in politics:

For too long, Christians have been so busy with the paramount work of making individuals right with God that they have let others do the business of politics and of government.... It's time today for Christians to move from their churches to the halls of Congress to bring about a change in the direction of this nation. For too long, Christians have seemed to think that politics was too dirty and messy for them to be involved in. I say that to the extent that politics is dirty and messy, the answer isn't to turn your back on it and walk away. It's to go out and get yourself a bar of soap and roll up your sleeves and make politics clean again. I think it's a Christian's duty to get involved in the political process. I think the big difference between·America today and the America of our founding fathers is not the lack of goodness in our people, but back then good Christian people were the ones who were doing the voting and the electing and the serving. Christians for many decades have sort of taken a sabbatical. It's time for them to get back and get involved...(and)...change the direction that America is traveling (Vander Jagt addressing National Affairs Briefing in Dallas, August 1980).

The dynamos behind the thrust of born-again politics are the televangelists. Whether or not they are engaging in direct advocacy of political involvement, most are constantly reminding their audiences of the collective sins of the nation and the need to repent.

There has been a great deal of confusion in the media about the New Right and the New Christian Right. Furthermore, many have failed to understand that the concept New Right does not refer to the resurgence of all the conservative forces in America, but rather to a fairly small group whose common bond is a mastery of the uses of modern communications technology. Almost without our recognizing it, modern communications technology has transformed politics from an art form into a science; an inexact science to be sure, but one in which the likely outcomes of alternative strategies can be estimated.

Consultants, advertising specialists, pollsters and direct-mail experts are the new kingmakers of American politics, having replaced the political bosses in the smoke-filled rooms of another era. Ironically, it was the efforts of a liberal congress to enact post-Watergate election reforms that give great momentum to the New Right. When election reforms cut out the fat cats, those who were experts at direct-mail fund raising took on greatly enhanced importance in American politics. Previously considered to be nickel-and-dime junk dealers by a lot of political pros, the direct-mail experts were able to demonstrate that by zeroing in on the right audience, a lot of little contributions could add up to big bucks.

All of the components of modern communications technology are now widely employed by Republicans and Democrats, conservatives and liberals alike. What has made the New Right an important force in American politics is that they got a big jump in mastering the technology. They have utilized it effectively to tap discontents and frustrations of that sector of society which then-Vice President Spiro Agnew labeled the "silent majority" back in the early 1970s. The active participation of the New Right in the political sweepstakes dates roughly to that period.

The New Right stands largely outside the party structures of American politics as well as the inner circles of power in Washington. Howard Phillips, who heads Conservative Caucus, is an exception. He was the architect of Richard Nixon's "southern strategy" and also the person Nixon tapped to dismantle Lyndon Johnson's "war on poverty" program. Whether he was the first among the New Right leadership to recognize the importance of drawing Christians into the conservative coalition, he certainly understood the importance of such a development. He has called the movement of conservative Christians into the political arena "the most significant development in American politics since organized labor discovered the ballot box."

The New Right sought to recruit television preachers into their movement for some time before they succeeded. They understood well the lessons of history. When you lock horns in social conflict, it's good to have God on your side. Your people fight harder and the opposition wilts more easily if your cause is godly. The liberals won the battle to define whose side God was on in the civil rights struggles of the 60s. Staking out the territory of life, family and country as their's has given conservatives some pretty good ammunition for the ensuing battles of the 80s. They frequently invoke the name of God as the progenitor of their cause, but they needed highly visible religious leaders to sanctify the invocation. The TV preachers could serve them well as legitimizers of their cause, but they could also mobilize their large conservative constituencies. So it happened that Jerry Falwell was sought out to create Moral Majority.

The New Christian Right owes its genesis to the master plan of the New Right. The New Right needs the New Christian Right to broaden its base of support and to render legitimate its causes. For the present, the New Christian Right needs the New Right, as the leadership of the former are no more than novices at big league politics. But they are fast learners and the New Right cannot long expect to equate their agendas with those of the New Christian Right unless the latter assents. The one big carrot the New Right has to offer conservatives to join their club is their command of modern communications technology. But this won't get them very far with the New Christian Right, for they have also been pioneers in this field. The modern communications technology which the New Right is using to transform American politics is essentially the same technology that the televangelists are using to build their religious empires. If they chose to use this same technology to develop political empires, there is nothing that can hold them to the New Right if they choose to go in other directions.

The National Affairs Briefing in Dallas provided crucial momentum for the emergence of the New Christian Right. The extensive news coverage announced to the nation the emergence of a budding social movement. News coverage begets coverage just as certainly as yeast leavens dough and television hits beget spin-offs and imitations. The media's discovery of these born-again politicians served also to legitimize their efforts to enter the political arena. While the notion that religion and politics don't mix is historically a myth, it had guided the consciousness of most evangelicals in recent history. Separation of church and state was one of the chief rhetorical weapons that conservative churches had to oppose the entanglement of liberal churches in civil rights during the 1960s.

Undoing old beliefs is not always easy. People have to be assured and reassured that the new beliefs or behavorial patterns are all right. Most of the evangelicals in America were not getting the message that involvements in politics is all right from watching religious programs on television. First, because the message that Christians should involve themselves in the political process was preached by only a few of the many television preachers. More importantly, a lot of evangelicals, perhaps a majority, never or seldom ever watch the TV preachers.

The news coverage served, thus, to draw attention to the efforts of a minority within evangelical ranks to draw the majority into the political arena. Sheer awareness of the fact that kindred souls are doing it provides confirming evidence that it might be all right. When one's own pastor becomes bold about political issues, the awareness that it is happening all over America may serve to cause people to listen rather than question the wisdom of his mixing of religion and politics. Even if they are not prepared to follow his invitation to become organizationally involved in politics, the fact that they choose not to oppose his engagement is an important step in legitimizing born-again politics. The shift from a generally negative or neutral posture toward the mixing of religion and politics, thus, is an important step in developing support for a broad-based movement.

The real importance of the Moral Majority and other New Christian Right organizations is not in what they accomplished during the 1980 elections, but rather in the *potential* they represent as a burgeoning social movement. There are three reasons this is so. First, there is much restlessness and discontent in America today and much of it is mobilizable in the name of Christian virtue. The number of evangelicals in America is large — very large. Second, every important social movement since television has been waged via mass communications. Marches and demonstrations are means to gain the attention of the news media and thereby bring the cause of social movement leaders into America's living rooms on the evening news. The New Christian Right doesn't have to draw a crowd to attract the attention of the media. They have merely to turn on their television cameras. The television preachers are not reaching the audiences they claim they are, but the audiences are sufficiently large to develop powerful social movement organizations. And when they want the rest of the country to pay attention, they can use their access to the airwaves to organize media events like *Washington for Jesus*.

The third factor that makes the potential of the New Christian Right so awesome is that they have mastered the use of the ancillary technology of television that pivots around the computer. Direct mail, targeted to audiences likely to be sympathetic to a cause, is the foundation. It is a proven way to raise big money and mobilize people to a cause.

In its infancy, modern communications technology sold us automobiles, beauty cosmetics, soap and beans. In its adolescence, it taught us to judge political candidates by their smile and clean presentation of self. Whether we are moving rapidly toward the worlds of mind control depicted by George Orwell in *1984* and Aldous Huxley in *Brave New World* isn't clear. Our world seems to possess greater quantities of complexity and ambiguity than appeared to be the case in these futuristic novels. But what does seem certain is that our consciousness will be shaped by the messages we receive via mass communications technology. The great struggle that is now shaping up is the struggle for access and control of that technology, for it is with this technology that the next great social movement will be waged.

The fury created by the movement of a few television preachers into politics during the 1980 campaign did not go away after the election because they are not going to go away and wait for the next election before they attempt to develop further political clout. What we are experiencing in America today is not the normal give and take of political parties that differ mainly in the mix of liberals and conservatives in their ranks.

The current struggle is more about the role of government in our lives; what it may and may not do, what it should and should not do and what it must and must not do. These concerns create a mosaic that criss-crosses traditional liberal-conservative positions. The answers any one ideological camp gives to the questions of how government may, should and must relate to our lives creates a kaleidoscope of incredible inconsistency. It is precisely for this reason that the upper hand held now by conservatives may not be decisive.

The countermobilization of persons and organizations standing in opposition to the New Christian Right is as natural a part of any social movement, as predictable as the rising and setting of the sun. And the greater the perceived threat of these right-wing Christians, the greater will be the effort to mobilize resources to attempt to check their political influence. What is not clear or predictable about this social movement and the establishment's counterinsurgency efforts, is the direction that both groups shall take.

To better understand the resurgence of conservative influence in America to date, one should focus on the New Right and its antecedents in 20th century conservativism in America. To understand where this movement is going, one needs to study carefully and watch the movements of the New Christian Right. It is the latter group that is likely to be responsible for shaping the next major developments in the move of conservatives to gain political power in America.

It is yet too early to know how all of this will turn out because the outcomes depend very much on decisions and alliances that have not yet occurred. The leadership of the electronic churches is only now beginning to be felt. If their role in the 1980 elections was exaggerated, the role they will play in the impending struggles may be decisive.

The outcome will determine the major thrust and direction of American society as we move into the 21st century. The struggle to determine whether we will enter the next century with determination to resolve the vexing dilemmas and problems that plague the U.S. and the industrial world or whether we shall drift ever closer to the abyss will be fought largely with modern communications technology. But some of the political alliances and outcomes of the struggle may be totally unanticipated in terms of the present alliances and caste of characters.

If Jerry Falwell doesn't have his finger on the pulse of the real moral majority in America, why shouldn't he gravitate toward those who could constitute the nucleus of a political consensus? When we reach the point that there is no escape from the realities of scarcity, then energy as well as other resources will be defined in moral-religious terms. If the current crop of television ministers fail to preach that message, they will lose their leadership to those who will. Television shapes our values, but it mirrors them as well.

The years just ahead are going to be very dangerous and anxious times for America and most of the world. Detente has come unstuck. With each passing year, the Middle East becomes more rather than less explosive. Most of the Third World is a time bomb with multiple fuses. Global economic collapse could be triggered from any number of events.

Such periods in history test the character of a people. Historically, when this nation has been tested, we have discovered deep moral fibers that have their roots in our pluralistic religious doctrines and principles. Our religious heritage has never been simplistic. As America has assimilated other cultures and religious perspectives over two centuries, the complexity of her collective faith has grown, even if its public expression has weakened. America may well be on the verge of another great religious awakening.

During the 1960s a small group of theologians pronounced the "death of God." But as so many scholars have noted, man is by nature a religious animal and does not exist without some form of religion. "It follows," Harvey Wheeler wrote, "that a death of God era is also a god-building era ... Our time is one of the most religious periods in all history, a time in which god-building is taking place at a dizzying pace" (Wheeler, 1971:8).

Eastern religions penetrated American culture in earnest during the late 1960s and since that time we have indeed experienced a proliferation of new religious expressions. But so also has this nation experienced sustained reexamination of traditional perspectives. Of all the religious ferment, there can be little question but that the growth of evangelistic faiths has been the largest and they have had the greatest immediate impact on our culture. But it may well be premature to assume monolithic political implications from what has transpired to date.

I don't quarrel with the general proposition that there is cause for concern about the potentially regressive influence they could have on American culture. But I do feel that those who are already hearing the thunderous boots of goose-stepping soldiers with swastika arm bands marching up Pennsylvania Avenue are overreacting. When Thomas Jefferson founded the University of Virginia, he wrote " ... we are not afraid to follow the truth wherever it may lead, nor to tolerate any error so long as reason is left free to combat it." There is a great core of good and common sense in America, a moral majority capable of struggling and coming to grips with the economic, political and moral imperatives of survival. They have survived the heavy diet of trash and pablum delivered on television since its birth. They will survive the manipulation and simplistic solutions to our problems that now are being offered by television preachers and politicians.

The struggle to reshape America will take place in front of us on our television sets. Television will not be simply the transmitter of news, but increasingly it will be the news as the cathode tube is utilized consciously to shape our consciousness. This will occur not only in explicitly religious programming, but in drama and investigative reporting. That the media seem primed, as never before, to transmit religious and moral messages may speak to the needs as well as the character of the American people.

REFERENCES

Armstrong, Ben. 1979. The Electric Church. Nashville: Thomas Nelson Publishers.

Bumpas, Frank. 1980. "Guidelines for Political Involvement." *Faith for the Family* 8/8:4-5.

Collins, Randall. 1975. Conflict Sociology. New York: Academic Press.

Rifkin, Jeremy. 1979. The Emerging Order. New York: G.P. Putnam's Sons.

Wheeler, Harvey. 1971. "The Phenomenon of God." *Center Magazine*. (March/April) 4:7-12.

IV

New Therapy

WHILE it is the least publicized, religion's role in the healing process may eventually prove to be the most significant new relevance of the sacred in secular society. The entanglement of religion and healing lies deep in the human experience, and religion's original and perhaps most fundamental relevance was its healing power. With the rise of scientific medicine, the healing arts were separated from their religious roots, and it appeared that religion had forever lost its therapeutic relevance. Such deep roots die hard, though, and the three papers in this section show that the "demedicalization" of religion has not killed its therapeutic potential or impulse.

Andrew Abbott's paper ("Religion, Psychiatry and Problems of Everyday Life") challenges conventional wisdom regarding the historical roles of clergy and physicians in dealing with personal problems. The medical secularization thesis assumes that psychiatrists literally displaced clergy as the high priests of psychological well-being in modern culture. But historical evidence from American society (1875-1935) does not support that belief, Abbott finds. Both clergy and other professionals handled such problems in the 19th century, and the rise of psychiatry did not curtail the clergy's role in this area. In the pastoral counseling movement, however, clergy abandoned their role as "saver of souls" for that of "counselor of personalities." If psychiatrists function as priests, Abbott suggests, it is only because clergy themselves have given up religious interpretations of everyday problems in favor of the psychiatric perspective. Instead of losing its therapeutic function, it appears religious therapy has simply been secularized.

Even that oversimplifies the matter, according to Long ("Religion and Therapeutic Action"), for in the same process, modern religion is resacralizing medical therapy. He views the adoption of the psychiatric perspective as part of a larger movement away from an emphasis on the "cure of souls" to the practice of what he calls "medical magic." That new model of therapeutic action combines secular medical premises with ancient magical practices around which the universal religions were first organized. This fusion of the sacred and secular gives religion certain adaptive advantages in advanced society, and Long speculates that it may define a new historic form of religion. If so, religion could well reclaim a central role for the sacred in modern healing and also establish a new reference point for human existence in advanced society.

The need for such a sacred reference point is emphasized in Michael Kearl's analysis of the modern response to aging ("Time, Identity and the Spiritual Needs of the Elderly"). Using a phenomenological approach to the study of meaning and identity in the life cycle, Kearl sees old age as a natural time for spiritual renaissance and for reaffirming the meaning of one's life. Until recently, religion had been the invisible framework for these tasks, but the secularization of time left the elderly without resources for biographical integration. Without religion, adjusting to old age became a problem for many individuals, and without that adjustment, social integration suffered as well. Secular society responded to those problems by employing "identity experts" to help plan and control the aging process. But without sacred backing, Kearl notes, their secular recipes for adjustment may be unable to satisfy the basic spiritual needs of the elderly.

8

RELIGION, PSYCHIATRY, AND PROBLEMS OF EVERYDAY LIFE

Andrew Abbott

PROBLEMS OF EVERYDAY LIFE IN THE 19TH CENTURY

It has become common to assert that psychiatrists are the priests of our time. By this it is usually meant that psychiatrists have acquired, from the clergy, the social function of the interpretation and control of individual problems with life. There are several elements to this view. First, clergy are assumed to have traditionally handled such problems. Second, psychiatrists are supposed by some process to have ousted them from this position. Third, a fairly constant set of problems concerning the meaning and nature of human life is taken as given. By analyzing a particular case, America from 1880 to 1930, I shall show that these assumptions are in fact mostly erroneous. Starting from a discussion of the traditional status of problems with everyday life, I shall then analyze clerical approaches to them. After contrasting these theories with psychiatric analyses of the same problems, I shall discuss changes in clerical practice in response to the expansion of psychiatric interests, and draw some conclusions about the implications of clergy involvement in this particular social problem.

In 1875 there was no general public conception of the problems of everyday life. *Angst* and maladjustment were not subjectively real categories of experience. People might have family or marital quarrels, career difficulties, financial problems, chronic minor illness, or even be generally unhappy. But these were seen as exigencies of life, not as encroachments on the highest level of personal functioning. These diverse problems of everyday life were handled by an equally diverse group of agents. Clearly family and friends played a major role. In addition, all of the professions seem to have dealt with them. Holmes's

The author thanks Harry Bredemeier, Susan Gal, Seward Hiltner, and Michael Moffatt for useful comments and criticisms.

novels show this clearly (Holmes, 1861). Doctor, lawyer, and clergyman were equally likely to guide an individual in personal difficulties. The warrant for such assistance was not professional knowledge, but rather the community status accorded to settled practitioners of the professions (Bailey, 1969; Barlow, 1898; Holmes, 1867; Long, 1937).

However, social changes in the late 19th century brought a new urgency to these everyday life problems. For men, especially of the upper and upper middle class, the period brought new opportunities for individualism—in careers, marriage, clubs, political and social groups. Yet social solidarity came increasingly to rest on personalities that could integrate this diversity (Durkheim, 1893; Simmel, 1955). There resulted a Babbitine choice between confusion and conformism. For women, the inverse problem of isolation became the focus of everyday life issues. Home life endured an effloration of etiquette and propriety (Schlesinger, 1946). Yet it also became a personal refuge from the difficulties of urban life (Sennett, 1970). Together these implied for women a different kind of anomie, an anomie of vacuity rather than of excess opportunity.

This qualitative change in the problems of everyday life was not met with effective changes in social control. Sociologists since Ross (1901) and Cooley (1909) have noted a decline in effective social controls with urban living. The Chicago school picture may have been overdrawn. Interstate mobility, family and household size, and even numbers of individuals on their own were surprisingly constant through the period. But the social disorganization analyzed by Park et al. (1925), Thomas and Znaniecki (1918) and others was not unusual. Family, neighborhood, church, and press, the traditional forces of primary social control, were not sufficient. The development of social work provides the clearest index of this failure, at least among the lower socioeconomic strata. At higher levels, the best evidence of failure is the enthusiasm that followed Beard's (1881) analysis of American nervousness in the eighties.

CLERGY RESPONSE

These changes in everyday life problems and their controls drew several responses from the clergy. Although these fall in rough chronological order, they overlap extensively. One cannot, therefore, view the clergy as responding to a "doctors' gambit" of neurasthenia, and then psychiatry responding to the clergy and so on back and forth. From 1895 to 1925 these issues were often debated and with quite diverse results. Therefore I shall first present the major views of both sides and then discuss the realities of professional jurisdictions.

The three clergy views discussed are all Protestant views. Data on Roman Catholics and Jews are meager.[1]

Even the Protestants left little on the subject of practice. Spencer (1858, 1865) is a notable exception. Fortunately, pastoral theology texts often discussed the writers' personal experiences. These can therefore give a preliminary guide, although the authors' desperate pleas for visitation imply a serious divergence between their theories and others' practice.[2]

One group of pastors defined personal troubles chiefly as occasions for *evangelism*. The pastor's duty was to find and nurture the religious meaning of a personal problem.

Seasons of sorrow in families are opportunities which ought to be carefully improved by ministers. The providence of God is then preparing the sufferers for the cordial reception of the blessings of the Gospel (Murphy, 1877:249).

These authors also insisted on regular visitation of all families, but generally for catechistical rather than pastoral purposes. This was not for children alone, nor was it necessarily a matter of stiff parlor talk.

It is well to sit down beside the wash-tub, or work bench, when necessary, and while work goes on direct the hearer's thoughts to heaven and to Christ (Bedell, 1880:410).

A second group, one that grew in numbers as the century closed, believed that *sympathy and support* were to come first. Willcox wrote:

Show your sympathy rather by simply pressing the sufferer's hand than by insisting prematurely on any Christian truth, however precious (Willcox, 1890:147).

Like the evangelistic group, this pastoral one urged routine visitation, but without the same catechistic intent. Instead they stressed the need of learning human nature, human suffering, human life and work. "In the morning of each day,' wrote Cuyler (1890), "study books: in the afternoon study doorplates and human nature."

Washington Gladden's writing on pastoral work forms a transition to a third view, which I shall call the *counseling* view. Pastoral work is to be founded on friendship. Its enemy is "unbending professionalism." Importantly, the rela-

[1] Among Jews, the rabbinate played a more formal, even judicial role, although the reform rabbinate drifted towards Protestant practices throughout this period (Carlin and Mendlovitz, 1958). For the Catholics, while one suspects an important clergy role in everyday life problems, the only data are official pronouncements that can tell little about actual practice.

[2] Although clergy diaries might seem an important source of information here, a survey of several potentially relevant diaries revealed no information whatever on the extent of pastoral work. Preaching and worship were the central foci. Doubtless intensive research would discover more information on pastoral function.

tion of affliction and salvation here becomes two way. While the pastor should know the social world in order to redeem it, yet redemption itself would be a cure for social problems.

How much there is, in every community, of anxiety and disappointment and heartbreaking sorrow that never comes to the surface .... The pastor has as little reason to complain of it as the doctor has to complain of a multiplicity of patients (Gladden, 1898:177).

In later years, the counseling theme of salvation as a cure of problems became more unabashed. K. R. Stolz wrote in 1932, "the higher integration and expansion of personality is the governing objective of modern Christian education and pastoral care" (Stolz, 1932:15). As for the old style of routine visiting, it "did make for the enlargement of the individual, although vast areas of personal difficulties remained untouched" (Ibid:18). By this time, Protestant clergy were acutely aware of the new problem of integration.

More people than ever, mothers and fathers and youth, are carrying burdens which a minister ought to share, and they are not apt to come to him in numbers if he does not care enough for them to go to them (McAfee, 1928:110).

Religion, evidently, was to be the cure.

PSYCHIATRIST'S RESPONSE

The changing problems of everyday life also brought diverse responses from the small psychiatric profession of the day. The first of these was the *nerves craze* of the eighties. Beard's *American Nervousness* (1881) delineated a syndrome of listlessness that many in the emerging nervous and mental disease specialty traced to the hectic pace of American life. As Haller and Haller (1974) and Gosling (1976) have argued, the profession's conceptions contained an explicit critique of everyday life in the gilded age, especially in the upper and upper middle class. Although the public furor died down, nervous ailments were a steadily increasing theme of the professional literature from this point on. (This can easily be seen by comparing numbers of articles listed on nerves and nervousness in Poole's on the one hand and Index Medicus on the other.) The underlying idea of this literature, as of the early 19th century theory of insanity, was that contemporary daily life overstrained the individual. As a result, nerves broke down in various ways. The implication, of course, was the necessity of a prevention, a theme that proved crucial in psychiatry's expansion out of the field of insanity.

The emphasis on prevention also characterized the second psychiatric response to everyday life problems, which focused on *social control*. Nervousness was not the only result of a hectic and strained life. Among the lower classes, psychiatrists argued, alcoholism, crime, juvenile delinquency, and illegitimacy were more likely. Such areas of social control became the intellectual frontiers of American psychiatry at the turn of the century, although most psychiatrists continued to practice with the insane and, to a lesser extent, the nervous.

Before 1900 heredity was usually identified as the chief cause of these problems, but increasingly they were attributed to the problems of daily life in modern society. While the Progressive Era at first believed that social change would eradicate the conditions creating those everyday problems, later years accepted the psychiatric insistence on personality as the crucial intervening variable (Lowrey and Sloane, 1948). This social control vocabulary entailed a general concept of adjustment that captured public opinion via the psychiatrically led mental hygiene movement (Deutsch, 1937). Describing its support of this approach, the Commonwealth Fund spoke of the need for research "into the complex causes—mental, physical, and social—of maladjustment in the individual . . . ." (1925-6:46). By 1930, the Fund was more explicit. "Psychiatry," it announced, "may do much to adjust human beings, children and adults, to tolerable conditions of life . . . ." (1930-1:52).

By the late twenties, however, parts of the psychiatric profession had carried to its logical extreme the idea that everyday life entailed *problems of adjustment*. This group, largely psychoanalytic, defined the personality in daily life as inherently problematic. The adjustment school had merely implied that everyone was maladjusted. The psychoanalysts believed it. The adjustment school had inched from the abnormal frontier in towards the core of normalcy. The analysts, both doctors and social workers, built from the inside out. Therapy came first for the therapist, only later for others (Reynolds, 1963; Van Waters, 1930). By reversing the order of cure, early American analysts created in theory and observed in practice the assumption that normal life was a disease to be cured. By doing this, they completed the psychiatric conception of the problem of everyday life. Since all were sick, life should be a progress toward a never-achieved "highest level of personal functioning." The scale, of course, was psychiatrically defined (Jahoda, 1958).

Psychiatry, therefore, was chiefly responsible for the creation and legitimation of a subjective category of personal *angst,* an anomic dissatisfaction that was seen as a chronic condition of modern living. Sociologists gave theoretical accounts of it, but psychiatrists defined it, treated it, explained it. It should be clear that they did not take it over from the clergy. First of all, the evidence indicates that many clergymen did their best to avoid dealing with everyday problems. Both routine and non-routine visitation were less frequent than the seminary instructors wished. Second, few clerical writers before 1900 saw everyday life problems as other than vehicles to salvation. Third, when the clergy did formulate a notion of the personal problems of modern life, in the counseling theory, it was drawn directly from psychiatric conceptions (Kolb, 1972).

CLERGY REACT

Changes in clergy practice, as opposed to theory, came in two waves. First were the clerical versions of *faith cure,* of which the Emmanuel Movement of Boston was the first (Meyer, 1965). Founded in 1906 by Elwood Worcester, an Episcopal priest with a PhD in psychology, this movement applied "the Christian religion as a healing power." Its goal was the

alleviation and arrest of certain disorders of the nervous system which are now generally regarded as involving some weakness or defect of character or more or less complete mental dissociation (Worcester and McComb, 1909:48).

The list of these disorders was given later in the same work:

nervous sufferers, victims of alcohol and other drugs, the unhappy, the sorrowful, would-be suicides, and other children of melancholy (Worcester and McComb, 1909:53).

The movement thus accepted medical definition of the new problem of integration (Gifford, 1974). Although the Emmanuel Movement was moribund by 1910, Harry Emerson Fosdick continued this tradition in the twenties when he asked the psychiatrist Thomas Salmon to consult with him on issues of pastoral counseling (Fosdick, 1943). Religion might help in the cure, but the disease itself was to be defined by the doctors. Here was the counseling view put into practice.

The second practical response by clergy to psychiatry attempted to *reassert religion's rights to define its own problems.* This movement grew out of Anton Boisen's experiences as mental patient (1920-1922) and as hospital chaplain (1924ff). Boisen invaded psychiatry to its very core, asking what was the religious meaning of the psychotic's ideas. Daring to ask this cost him several extra months under psychiatric supervision in the Westboro State Hospital (Boisen, 1960). But Boisen also insisted that ministers must deal with the grave religious problems of everyday life. These lay not in failure to reach a highest level of personal functioning, but rather in being "unawakened."

These are persons usually fairly well adjusted in the vocational, social or sexual fields, who have never really come to terms with their ultimate loyalties. They are those who, passively accepting the faith of their fathers, make no determined effort to bring themselves into conformity with its requirements, but go through life absorbed all too often in the petty, the trivial, the selfish, or even in that which makes them loathesome in their own eyes. I am ready ... to recognize that in order that they may turn and be made whole it may be necessary to disturb their conscience in regard to the quality of life they are living (Boisen, 1936:280).

Boisen insisted on defining everyday life as problematic not for its unhappiness, but for its triviality. As in the earlier evangelistic view, everyday problems, like the psychoses, were merely occasions for the posing of religious questions. Yet Boisen's lead was not followed. The movement for clinical pastoral education that he started (with Russell Dicks and Richard Cabot) eventually drifted towards the counselors' theory of religion as therapy (Hiltner, 1958, 1978). Boisen's personal students, such as Seward Hiltner, have continued in the evangelistic tradition. But the movement, institutionalized in the Council for the Clinical Training of Theological Students in 1930, retreated to the pastoral position rapidly (Kemp, 1947). Clinical training would teach the seminarian the rudiments of human nature. Importantly, the definition of those rudiments was in the hands of the psychiatrists, psychologists, and social workers with whom the student was to learn to cooperate. In more recent years the pastoral counseling movement has split off from the parish clergy altogether in the founding of the American Association for Pastoral Counseling (1963). Curiously, this had been predicted by Parsons (1960) on purely functional grounds.

ANALYSIS AND CONCLUSIONS

The common theory that psychiatry displaced the clergy as custodians of everyday life problems should thus be qualified. At the level of professional theories, the psychiatrists invented the modern version of the everyday life problem. Boisen's religious approach to it has had little influence. The pastoral counseling movement was in fact the clergy's involvement in that social problem as psychiatrically defined. For whatever reason, the major thinkers of the movement came to view religion as a means to personal happiness rather than as a meaning system in itself. The few who insisted on meaning were ignored. Therefore, the clergy involvement in this social problem has implied a decline in clergy involvement with religion.

At the level of practice, both professions dealt with everyday problems from the beginning of the period here discussed. Yet the clerical presence was probably the stronger throughout. Although obligations for visiting were often ignored by clergy, the early psychiatrists were a tiny group reaching little of the population. Even by 1916, when a speaker at the American Medico-Psychological Association annual meeting estimated that the average neurologist spent half of his time working with psychological problems, the psychiatric influence was chiefly theoretical, not practical (Clark, 1916). Yet the clergy were surprisingly inactive, as perhaps laymen expected them to be. Pastoral work was conspicuously absent, for example, from the concerns of the Interchurch World Movement, a major postwar revival effort (Interchurch World Movement, 1920). Nonetheless, given that there were in 1920 one hundred-forty clergymen for every psychiatrist in private practice, an individual was still much more likely to take personal problems to a clergyman or possibly, as in the nineteenth century, to a non-specialist physician. In practice, then, the formation and development of the psychiatric profession did not really affect the clergyman's place in handling personal problems. Dexter and Dexter (1931) report an increase in such work among clergy by the thirties. The independent impact of the new self-help associations, of the social work profession, and of the mental hygiene movement is beyond the scope of this paper. In general, however, their effect was to make the clergyman a front line professional identifying and referring personal problems to specialists.

As a description of a concrete historical process, then, the theory that psychiatrists have assumed the clergy role of controlling problems with everyday life rests on insufficient foundations. First, the clergy shared jurisdiction over everyday life problems with other professions during the nineteenth century. Second, clergy practice with such problems was not radically curtailed by psychiatric practice, since the disparity in numbers was so great. Third, the clergy's new interest in everyday life problems after the turn of the century was largely a response to psychiatric work redefining these problems. The basic assumptions of the replacement theory—original clergy jurisdiction, psychiatric displacement, and constant problems—are thus rejected. Yet the last of these, the assumption that everyday life problems were constant throughout, suggests by its failure the sense in which the "inheritor theory" is correct.

Functional theorists of religion (Geertz, 1965) argue that religion is the cultural system that gives ultimate conceptions of the order of things and clothes them with absolute reality. In the nineteenth century evangelistic theory of personal problems, the ultimate reality was, of course, the Christian drama of sin and redemption. Everyday life problems might be a means to that religious end. In the twentieth century psychoanalytic theory, the minimization of personal unhappiness (or, in the ego psychology revision, the raising of an individual to his highest level of functioning) became the end in itself. Hence the psychiatric redefinition of the everyday life problems involved a movement of those problems from the periphery of one ultimate meaning system to the very center of another. The true psychiatric replacement of the clergy was thus not a replacement of clerical practice with such problems, but rather a replacement of the clerical interpretation of them as ancillary to the ultimate ends of life. If psychiatrists are the priests of our time, it is not because they have displaced the clergy from practice with the individual problems of life, but rather because they (and others) have persuaded the culture that personal realization is indeed the ultimate end of life. In the functional sense of defining ultimate meaning and order, the psychiatrists may indeed be our true religious officials.

The fallacy with which we began is thus a fallacy of hypostatization—functional replacement does not require a concrete historical process of displacement. In fact, the true historical process was more one of clergy abandonment of the interpretative role, as we have here seen. In the years since 1930, little has changed on this score. Clergy efforts to seek independent, religious models for the meaning of modern *angst* seem far outweighed by the emergence of pastoral counseling as another lay avatar of psychiatry. In fact, this abandonment of religion's interpretative task was clear by the thirties. Carroll Wise spoke for the mainstream of the growing movement for "clinical training" in pastoral work when he wrote in 1942:

The clergyman must have a living faith to express through his methods. This involves not only the "religion" of the clergyman, but his total personality and his cultural relationships. In other words, the clergyman cannot hide behind symbols which mean little or nothing to his congregation and expect to make a significant contribution to modern life ... Students emerging from the average theological school today may be experts in Biblical criticism, in philosophical or theological argument ... .But they are not trained to deal with the fundamental material of the ministry—the human personality. Their thinking becomes book-centered, idea-centered, or program-centered, whereas it should be centered in the personality (Wise, 1942:262-3).

The shift from saver of souls to counselor of personalities was thus ideologically complete from the earliest years of the current movement for clinical training of clergy. The mechanisms by which it created a new professional subspecialty, the non-parochial clergy counselor, must remain a topic for further research.

References

Bailey, Percival. 1969. Up From Little Egypt. Chicago: Buckskin.

Barlow, C. 1898. Daydreams of a Doctor. Buffalo: Peter Paul.

Beard, George M. 1881. American Nervousness: Its Causes and Consequences. New York: Putnam.

Bedell, Gregory T. 1880. The Pastor: Pastoral Theology. Philadelphia: Lippincott.

Boisen, Anton T. 1936. The Exploration of the Inner World. Chicago: Willet, Clark.

1960. Out of the Depths. New York: Harper.

Carlin, J. E., and S. H. Mendlovitz. 1958. "The American Rabbi." In M. Sklare (ed.). The Jews: Social Patterns of an American Group. Glencoe, Ill.: Free Press.

Clark, L. Pierce. 1916. "Extra-Asylum Psychiatry." Transactions of the American Medico-Psychological Association 73:373-377.

Commonwealth Fund. 1925-26. Annual Report. New York: Commonwealth Fund.

Commonwealth Fund. 1930-31. Annual Report. New York: Commonwealth Fund.

Cooley, Charles Horton. 1909. Social Organization. New York: Scribners.

Cuyler, Theodore L. 1890. How to Be a Pastor. New York: Baker and Taylor.

Deutsch, Albert. 1937. The Mentally Ill in America. New York: Columbia.

Dexter, Elizabeth W. and Robert C. Dexter. 1931. The Minister and Family Troubles. New York: Richard R. Smith.

Durkheim, Emile. 1893. The Division of Labor in Society. Tr. by George Simpson. New York: Free Press (1964).

Fosdick, Harry E. 1943. On Being a Real Person. New York: Harper.

Geertz, Clifford. 1965. "Religion as a Cultural System." In M. Banton (ed.). Anthropological Approaches to the Study of Religion. London: Tavistock.

Gifford, Sanford. 1974. The Emmanuel Movement, Medical Psychotherapy, and the Battle over Lay Treatment, 1906-1912. Unpub. Ms.

Gladden, Washington. 1898. The Christian Pastor and the Working Church. New York: Scribners.

Gosling, Francis G. 1976. American Nervousness: A Study in Medicine and Social Values in the Gilded Age, 1870-1900. Unpub. PhD Dissertation. Norman: University of Oklahoma.

Haller, John S. and Robin M. Haller. 1974. The Physician and Sexuality in Victorian America. New York: Norton.

Hiltner, Seward. 1958. A Preface to Pastoral Theology. New York: Abingdon.

1978. Personal Communication.

Holmes, Oliver Wendell, Sr. 1861. Elsie Venner. Boston: Ticknor and Fields.

1867. The Guardian Angel. Boston: Ticknor and Fields.

Interchurch World Movement. 1920. World Survey, Vol. 1. America. New York: Interchurch Press.

Jahoda, Marie. 1958. Current Concepts of Positive Mental Health. New York: Basic.

Kemp, Charles F. 1947. Physicians of the Soul. New York: MacMillan.

Kolb, Frances A. 1972. The Reaction of American Protestants to Psychoanalysis, 1900-1950. Unpub. PhD Dissertation. St. Louis, Missouri: Washington University.

Long, Francis A. 1937. A Prairie Doctor of the Eighties. Norfolk, Nb: Huse.

Lowrey, Lawson G. and Victoria Sloane. 1948. Orthopsychiatry, 1923-1948: Retrospect and Prospect. American Orthopsychiatric Association.

McAfee, Cleland B. 1928. Ministerial Practices. New York: Harper.

Meyer, Donald B. 1965. The Positive Thinkers. Garden City, New York: Doubleday.

Murphy, Thomas. 1877. Pastoral Theology. Philadelphia: Presbyterian Board of Publication.

Park, R. E., E. W. Burgess, and R. D. McKenzie. 1925. The City. Chicago: University of Chicago Press.

Parsons, Talcott. 1960. "Mental Illness and 'Spiritual Malaise': the Role of the Psychiatrist and of the Minister of Religion." In Hans Hoffman (ed.). The Minister and Mental Health. New York: Association Press.

Reynolds, Bertha C. 1963. An Uncharted Journey. New York: Citadel.

Ross, Edward A. 1901. Social Control. New York: MacMillan.

Schlesinger, Arthur M., Sr. 1946. Learning How to Behave. New York: MacMillan.

Sennett, Richard. 1970. Families Against the City. Cambridge, Mass.: Harvard.

Simmel, Georg. 1955. Conflict and the Web of Group Affiliations. Tr. by Kurt Wolff and Reinhard Bendix. New York: Free Press.

Spencer, Ichabod S. 1858. A Pastor's Sketches, New York: Dodd.

1865. A Pastor's Sketches: second series. New York: Dodd.

Stolz, Karl R. 1932. Pastoral Psychology. Nashville: Cokesbury.

Thomas, W. I. and Florian Znaniecki. 1918. The Polish Peasant in Europe and America. (1918-1920). Boston: Badger.

Van Waters, Miriam. 1930. "Philosophic Trends in Modern Social Work." In Fern Lowry (ed.). Readings in Social Casework. New York: Columbia.

Willcox, Giles B. 1890. The Pastor Amidst His Flock. New York: American Tract Society.

Wise, Carroll A. 1942. Religion in Illness and Health. New York: Harper.

Worcester, Elwood and Samuel McComb. 1909. The Christian Religion as a Healing Power. New York: Moffat, Yard.

9

RELIGION AND THERAPEUTIC ACTION: FROM HEALING POWER TO MEDICAL MAGIC

Theodore E. Long

Systematic sociological exploration of the relation of religion and healing in the modern world has only barely begun. As yet unsure of the terrain, recent expeditions into this uncharted territory have relied on the familiar secularization hypothesis as a provisional guide to inquiry (McGuire, 1981). That perspective assumes the functional differentiation of religion and healing, the latter now located in the realm of scientific medicine. Modern religion now specializes in providing personal meaning in an otherwise rationalized world and more specifically, in comforting souls troubled by "secular" illness. Thus religion can influence the action of physicians (Crane, 1975) or provide a framework for understanding the nonmedical aspects of illness (Shriver, 1980). For its part, medicine may try to medicalize (deviant) religion as mental illness of some sort (Robbins and Anthony, 1982). Religious healing, once a principal expression of religion and the dominant form of healing, is now located at the margins of the territory in sectarian or cultic groups and in nonmodern religious traditions (Moody, 1974; Harwood, 1977; Bainbridge, 1978).

There are two related problems with this approach, one methodological, the other substantive. Methodologically, it permits secular medicine to define the relevance of religion in matters of healing; whatever medicine claims as part of its domain is excluded from religion's. That strategy deflects attention from religion's own claims on the healing enterprise, which have always been a central part of its mission, no less in today's secular age than in the past.

This is a revised version of a paper originally prepared for the Annual Meeting of the Association for the Sociology of Religion, August, 1981, Toronto, Canada. I have benefited from the comments of Todd Hanson and Steve Kent, and I am grateful for the research assistance of David Kraueter, Lynn Guyeska and Sue Standard.

Substantively, current approaches overlook what appears to be a resacralization of medicine as advanced medical technology reaches its limits and confronts ultimate questions (Fox, 1979). That development challenges the secularization approach to religion and healing and opens the complementary possibility that modern religion may be appropriating medicine for its own healing efforts.

In this paper I examine religion's historic orientation(s) to healing in relation to the secularization thesis. The investigation shows that contemporary western religion has adopted a new model of healing, which takes the character of *medical magic applied to the everyday life problems of individuals*. The model represents both the secularization of religion and the "reenchantment" of secular medicine. To the extent that this paradoxical orientation comes to guide religious action, it may also define a new stage in the historic development of religion itself. To expose these trends and possibilities I rely on two theoretical typologies: Weber's (1963) analysis of the historic modes of religious action, and Siegler and Osmond's (1974) outline of the models of therapeutic action. A brief summary of their ideas will lay the groundwork for my historical review of religion's healing practice.

MODELS OF ACTION: RELIGIOUS AND THERAPEUTIC

Religious Action. Weber developed his sociology of religion around the distinction between *magic and religion,* categories he used both as ideal types and as stages in religious evolution. As methods of dealing with the supernatural, both constitute genuine forms of religious action, which Weber characterizes as follows.

The relationships of men to supernatural forces which take the forms of prayer, sacrifice and worship may be termed 'cult' and 'religion,' as distinguished from 'sorcery,' which is magical coercion. Correspondingly, those beings that are worshipped and entreated religiously may be termed 'gods,' in contrast to 'demons,' which are magically coerced and charmed (p.28).

Magic is strictly instrumental action which seeks by the application of ritual formulae to appropriate supernatural power for the satisfaction of specific human needs and desires of the most mundane variety. In religion, by contrast, humans submit themselves to the guidance of the supernatural throughout the life course, using ritual to worship the god(s), to make entreaties to them, and to receive their "revelation." All religious action has its roots in and incorporates some magic, but religious evolution moves toward "religion" as the dominant form of action. Several features of this distinction between magic and religion are worth highlighting here.

1. Because it aims to achieve practical goals in this world, magic is characterized by a *"calculating rationalism"* (p. 27), based on human knowledge and skill in manipulating the supernatural (cf. Hammond, 1970). In contrast, religion is irrational, that is, *noncalculating,* because it is "For God" rather than "For Man" (Schneider, 1974). In religion, for example, ritual is valued in itself as an expression of the faith, but in magic, ritual has no value unless it produces certain specific, tangible effects.

2. At the same time, however, religion involves "a *rational systematization* of the god concept" (p. 27). In this respect, magic is *nonrational,* for it deals with problems on an *ad hoc* basis and confronts arbitrary spirits.

3. That difference shows up concretely in the normative rules emphasized in each type. Magic is associated with an assortment of specific *taboos* developed in response to the arbitrary action of the spirits (p. 37ff.). The hallmark of religion, on the other hand, is a rational system of *ethics* operative in all life situations and to which adherents are routinely held accountable.

4. Magic and religion also differ in the status and power of their gods. Magical spirits or demons all have unusual power, but it is usually specialized and vulnerable to corresponding weaknesses, which makes them *manipulable.* The god(s) of religion, though, tend to be *omnipotent* and *omniscient,* thus far less responsive to manipulation than to entreaty and supplication.

5. A further difference concerns the administration of religious action. Magicians and sorcerers are *independent operators* whose standing depends solely on their personal gifts of charisma and ritual efficacy. Religion, in contrast, relies on *priests* who specialize "in the continuous operation of a cultic enterprise, permanently associated with particular norms, places and times, and related to specific social groups" (p. 30). Regular pastoral care, which Weber defines as "the religious cultivation of the individual," is the "priests' real instrument of power ... over the workaday world" (p. 75).

6. The medial figure between magician and priest who stimulates the movement toward religion is the *prophet.* Like the magician, the prophet "exerts his power simply by virtue of his personal gifts. Unlike the magician, however, the prophet claims definite revelations, and the core of his mission is doctrine or commandment, not magic" (p. 47). What makes the prophet believable is his magical work; what he asks people to believe is a new or renewed religion.

Therapeutic Action. Like Weber, Siegler and Osmond organize their analysis of therapeutic action around a central dichotomy, that between *continuous* and *discontinuous* models of madness. Though originally formalized to study psychiatric approaches to mental illness, these models have been applied to the whole range of personal problems and physical disorders by medical and nonmedical therapists alike. Each incorporates a different view of human misfortune and what can be done to alleviate it. Continuous models "offer an inclusive global view of human destiny in which our various misfortunes play a large part" (p. 42). Misfortune is an expression of the cosmos gone awry, the manifestation of larger forces which ultimately control all human life. One cannot alleviate the misfortune without altering the operation of those cosmic forces. Discontinuous models, on the other hand, "put forth a partial or restricted rather than a global view of the problem," which is treated in "an immediate but limited way .... There is no attempt at a total explanation or solution for the whole" (p. 21). The focus is on achieving "practical solutions to particular crises" (p. 21).

The chances for therapeutic success differ according to the definition of the problem. In continuous models, success is hard to come by, and at the extreme, there is often a belief that nothing can be done. In discontinuous models success is so much more likely that it is almost taken for granted, to the point that sometimes treatment is pursued even when there is little real chance of success. "In consequence, the affect of those using continuous models is usually serious and even gloomy. Its tone is fundamentally religious, in contrast to the secular cheerfulness of those employing the discontinuous models" (p. 43).

In both types, therapeutic action is undertaken by experts able to discern the source of trouble and to combat it. On the basis of that expertise, they claim authority to diagnose and treat patients according to medical prerogative. In fact, however, their claims to authority rest on quite different grounds. Those using discontinuous models ground their expertise in empirical scientific knowledge. Those using continuous models rely instead on revelation and insight which comes from personal experience or sensitivity. The authority of continuous therapists, then, is quite personal, almost charismatic in Weber's sense, while discontinuous authority rests on an organized community of colleagues who contribute to, believe in, and rely on a common system of rational knowledge, like priests. But unlike religious action, where magical calculation is divorced from religious systematization, the different types of rationality are here consistently joined. Based on rationally systematized knowledge, discontinuous therapy also displays a calculating, instrumental orientation, using demonstrated formulae for achieving concrete treatment objectives. Continuous therapeutic action is distinctly irrational, being concerned less with effectiveness than with being "right."

Siegler and Osmond identify five continuous and three discontinuous models, several of which require brief comment here. The most prominent continuous model is the "psychoanalytic," which seems often to come close to the Christian theology of sin and human failing. Also noteworthy is the "social" model, which views misfortune as symptomatic of a sick society. Siegler and Osmond focus on those views which emphasize poverty and discrimination, but any social malady could find a place here. On the discontinuous side they locate what they believe to be the true "medical" model, which focuses on the differential diagnosis and treatment of measurable sickness. What we call the "moral" model is also discontinuous, but it is not what we usually think of as a religious morality which emphasizes inherent sinfulness and the drama of salvation and damnation. Rather, it is really the behaviorist paradigm for changing unacceptable behavior.

FROM HEALING POWER TO MEDICAL MAGIC

With these frameworks in mind, consider the role of healing in western Christianity. There we can see three distinct conceptions of healing ministry: (1) healing power, (2) the cure of souls, and (3) medical magic. That sequence represents the historical order of their development and dominance in religious practice. Dominance, however, does not imply exclusivity; preceding modes of action usually persist to some extent in succeeding stages.

Healing Power. The Christian religion originated in the charismatic prophecy of Christ, a classic example of Weber's prophet type. As a charismatic leader, Jesus' authority rested on his providing concrete signs of his alleged gifts and divinity, which he accomplished in a series of miracles. Not all of these miracles were healing, but a great number were, and healing took a prominent place in Christ's conception of his mission and in his commandments to his followers. To "heal the sick, raise the dead, cleanse the lepers, cast out devils" (Matthew 10:7) were primary components of his ministry.

Despite the church's subsequent claims to the contrary, these healing miracles were clearly magical, as Smith (1978) has so carefully shown. They appropriated great supernatural power for discrete, practical aims as the need arose. In particular, Jesus healed people afflicted with specific physical ailments or possessed by demons, the analogue to mental illness. There was no elaborate theology of healing or any pretense that it had any greater significance. It was simply a raw show of power over the natural world, other sorcerers, and the old spirits in which people believed. In exchange for that show of healing power, Jesus exacted an expression of faith in him and his god, a bargain on which the church built a more universalistic religion—and eventually its system of medical magic.

Reliance on healing power as a central component of Christian mission persisted into the middle ages. The church was fighting the masses' tendency to rely on nonchristian magic, and the claim to healing power was its main weapon against those competitors (McGuire, 1981). At the same time, though, "magic ... was savagely condemned by churchmen" as a "perversion of proper forms of devotion" and as a false claim "to compel supernatural forces'' (Peters, 1978 xvi). That critique arose as part of Christianity's movement toward universalistic religion, which supported a new model of healing, the cure of souls. For all its historic momentum, that development was not fully completed until scientific medicine overcame belief in supernatural forces as agents of disease and healing. Even then, the magical idea of healing power persisted, and it reappears regularly in marginal sects and nonmodern traditions.

Cure of Souls. Under cover of the healing power paradigm, the Christian church had been developing a more generalized theology of healing which focused on the ultimate reconciliation of sinful people with God. Human illness was a flaw in creation created by sin, and God's purpose in the world was to eradicate sin and to create a perfect kingdom. Healing particular illnesses was but one small aspect of that process, the ultimate aim of which was eternal salvation. Healing was thus conceived in more comprehensive terms as a process of reconciling people to God. It infused every sphere of life with ultimate significance so that the soul became the focus of religious healing. Correspondingly, the pastoral care of individual believers was the preeminent method of cure for sinful souls. That work consisted primarily in bringing all aspects of individual life under the influence and care of religious precepts through interpretation, teaching, accountability and judgment (cf. McNeil, 1951).

Part of the church's struggle with the magic of the masses pivoted around its interest in the cure of souls. Magical folk healing was at philosophical odds with this rational theology, which could not be effectively implemented until that magic was discredited. Ironically, so long as it monopolized healing under supernatural aegis, the church needed the magic of healing power to justify its more intangible claim to cure souls. Only with the rise of medicine as a secular healing power was the church able to relinquish its own claims in that domain and center its healing primarily on the cure of souls, for the magic of the masses had been overcome. The foundations for that shift were in place by the 17th century, but it was not fully completed until the 18th and 19th centuries (Moore, et. al, 1980:231ff.).

As Harrell makes clear in the case of Protestant America, these developments "increasingly separated healing (of body and mind) from religion ... but most Protestant leaders did not feel threatened by these intrusions'' (1980: 63-4, parentheses added). In fact, he notes, Protestant theologians "embraced and used'' science as another expression of religious truth, and they ceded responsibility and authority for physical healing to physicians as specialized agents in the larger program of the cure of souls. Though it took somewhat longer, medicine gradually gained hegemony over mental illness as well.

The ministry of curing souls took two different directions: *individual pietism* under watchful pastoral care and *social ministry* to cure society of its ills. At first, social ministries seemed little more than an extension of personal piety as the church reached out to save wayward souls who disrupted social harmony (alcoholics, orphans, etc.). Over time, however, social ministry became more critical of established order and emphasized social reform at the expense of individual salvation. The well-known historical rift in American Protestantism between pietists (conservatives) and reformers (liberals) which grew out of these trends was real enough. But what we often overlook is how deeply both relied on the common therapeutic urge to cure souls—their own. Both saw their efforts as duties to religious commands, whose fulfillment was necessary as a step toward their own salvation. In Weber's terms, both shared an ascetic orientation to the problem of resolving discrepancies between religion's demands and worldly conditions. The pietists had simply preferred the other-worldly solution, while the reformers concentrated on this world. That this conflict has persisted so long and so bitterly at times testifies to the power of self-justificatory motives and needs in the curing of the soul.

The same forces which permitted the cure of souls to flourish as a healing strategy eventually (and inevitably) undermined it. In ceding control of physical and mental illness to medicine, religion had abandoned the ground on which it had built its reputation and authority. To maintain its legitimacy and plausibility, religion required some visible success, but success in the eternal cure of souls was both harder to achieve and less convincing than the more tangible successes of medicine. It took some time for the balance to shift, during which religion prospered, but gradually medical success overcame religious ambiguity and the social authority of religion—even in the cure of souls—began to wane.

Medical Magic. While most observers focused on religion's decline in the process of secularization, both established churches and new religious groups were experimenting with a new healing model that would eventually blossom into a program of medical magic. For example, Johnson (1981) points out that almost all popular religious movements of the last century focused on "The therapeutic transformation of the self" (p. 51) in which "the problems of personal life" (p. 52) would be overcome. Included among these movements were such otherwise diverse faiths as pentecostal groups and oriental philosophies. In the established church, Abbott (1980) notes, clergy adopted the psychiatric conception of "everyday life problems" (p. 164) as a special type of malady which could be cured religiously. Even before the turn of the century, some of them began to revise their view of the pastor's role "from saver of souls to counselor of personalities" (p. 170). By the 1930s, movements to establish "clinical training" in seminaries had been launched (Larson, 1980), and Clinical Pastoral Education has now become a central part of ministerial training in many church bodies, including Episcopalians, Presbyterians, Lutherans and Southern Baptists. In that process, Abbott suggests, religion abandoned its role as the primary definer and interpreter of ultimate meaning for the apparently more profitable and productive one of curing tangible individual problems of daily life.

The movement toward medical magic proceeds along two main lines today. The primary developments are taking place within religious organizations, the old and new alike. Many new religions, such as The Power (Bainbridge, 1978), Scientology (Bainbridge and Stark, 1980) and Transcendental Meditation are famous for their therapeutic bent. They make self-improvement via therapeutic means a major part of their activity, often to the point that it eclipses theology as the defining characteristic of the group.

Less visible but far more immense, is the similar movement in established churches, where a religious version of psychiatric theory has taken firm hold. That "theology" emphasizes the universal tendency of the modern world to debilitate individuals through stress, anxiety, insoluble dilemmas, perpetual conflict, and the like (cf. Abbott, 1980). These are not special misfortunes which befall a few poor souls, but natural components of ordinary life for everyone. Neither are they limited to the private realm of life. To be sure, private relations are prominent, especially family relations (cf. Telleen, 1980), but the real rub comes from public life, where work and political relations impose a constant strain on each of us. As Johnson suggests, these theories accept the conclusion that "the anarchy of work is reflected in intimate relationships. The logic of the workplace has invaded the bedroom" (1981: 55). To combat these ills, the church offers its own therapeutic, the end of which is not salvation but "peace of mind," "feeling better about oneself," "meaningful fellowship," "coping," and "answers to your problems." The eternal fate of people's souls becomes a secondary concern. First and foremost, it is tangible help for the self in the here and now that the churches promote as their *raison d'etre*.

Those who believe that such secular trends attract only liberals often overlook the degree to which the conservative traditions have also adopted this approach. For example, the pastor of a large Southern Baptist congregation in Virginia has a one-minute radio spot every day called "God's Minute." He begins by posing some perplexing problem arising from daily living, and then he offers his cure: come to church on Sunday. The clear implication is that coming to church is good therapy; hellfire and damnation have fallen by the wayside. A more prominent example is found on television among the fundamentalist and evangelical "prime-time preachers" (Hadden and Swann, 1981). There cures for everyday problems are passed out by the dozens, and thousands more are promised through prayer if only the viewer will call or write—and of course, contribute. Liberals and conservatives alike appear to have substituted therapy for theology, just like new religions.

The second prong of this therapeutic movement in religion is more specialized, less well-developed, and found primarily in established churches. That is the effort to associate religious therapy with medical treatment in the cure of physical and mental disease. Here the premise is that treating disease alone is insufficient for the person. Along with disease come various other afflictions, of the same variety as everyday life problems, and religion is better able to treat them than medicine. The most prominent example of this trend is the Wholistic Health Movement, which aims at the creation of teams of physicians, social workers, clergy and others to treat the whole person, not just the disease alone (Westberg, 1980). A related effort involves the attempt to incorporate religiously based principles into medical training itself to prepare physicians to deal with the total person (Shriver, 1980).

These new healing practices bear remarkable resemblance to magic, as Weber typifies it. They are, first of all, unabashedly oriented to the accomplishment of tangible ends in this world. Unlike Weber's "this worldly religion," where eternal salvation is the overarching aim of worldly effort, the new medical magic virtually abandons the hope of salvation for the sake of personal peace on earth. Second, these practices are clearly instrumental, displaying a calculating orientation to the achievement of practical ends, and they depend on rational formulae to accomplish them. Third, the image of God which accompanies these practices clearly departs from that of the universalistic world religions. Today's gods are chastened by the success of secular enterprise, such as medicine. They have power, but they are not omnipotent, and there are some things they cannot do. Finally, many religious leaders, particularly in the new religious groups and in conservative churches (including TV preachers), have taken on the role of wizards and sorcerers, much like the magical times of old.

But if this is magic, it is not pure magic. In most established churches, pastoral care is still emphasized, as in Weber's "religion." The pastor's role is changing more to that of expert counselor, but it remains more characteristic of Weber's "priest," though now a "facilitating" priest rather than an "authoritative" one (cf. Goetting, 1980). Likewise, religious knowledge is still rationally systematized, unlike the magician's lore, though much of it is now secular knowledge. Finally, religious healing still maintains at least the form of a religious ethic, as opposed to a series of arbitrary taboos, even though these ethical principles are being rotated toward a view of them as guidelines for healthy living.

What holds this unlikely combination of traits together is religion's peculiar appropriation of the medical model. With one hand, religion holds to a continuous theory of disease which emphasizes the global source of individual problems and the universal misfortune that befalls us all in modern society. In its most prominent version, the churches' approach is reminiscent of Siegler and Osmond's "social" model of madness, though it has been broadened somewhat. Those who work to make religious healing an adjunct of medicine typically rely on a watered down version of the psychoanalytic model. With the other hand, however, religion offers a discontinuous solution, one with all the earmarks of the specific model Siegler and Osmond call "medical." It adopts the medical principle of authority by reliance on scientific knowledge as a basis of expertise, and it uses the medical paradigm of diagnosis and treatment for specific ills.

That combination poses a problem of logical consistency, but religion has developed a resourceful solution to it. The fact that people will suffer at the hands of the world is taken to be inevitable and never-ending. But the particular misfortune that befalls each individual at specific times is variable, needs specific diagnosis, and can profit by treatment. The catch, and it is a rather elegant one, is that successful treatment will not prevent further misfortune. Indeed, further misfortune is sure to befall us all; so everyone must keep returning to receive therapy. Thus does religion maintain its analogue to original sin and its conquering power, only now it presumably has something to show for its efforts.

MEDICAL MAGIC, SECULARIZATION AND RELIGIOUS EVOLUTION

What we have, it appears, is a new form of religious action, not exactly magic and not exactly "religion," but something which combines elements of each with portions of secular medicine. Whether that unusual hybrid can flourish and sustain itself is an open question, but there is good reason to believe it will. As a practical matter, magic shows usually draw crowds, and if the sorcerer is any good at all, new followers and their money as well. Today, success need not be even that uncertain, for practitioners can be trained readily and reliably in the practice of this modern magic. It helps, in addition, that scientific medicine can produce enough cures and remissions to sustain belief in its potency but not so many as to dispel its mysterious and aweful character. Organizationally and politically, it offers both to heal the rift between pietists and reformers in Protestantism and to underwrite rapprochement between Protestants and Catholics, established churches and new religions. That opportunity exists because medical magic seizes upon the common human interest in health and illness which sustained the "church universal" in its prime. To use religious language, it begins with "man's experience" rather than with "God's commands."

To say that already anticipates the more historic significance of medical magic, which comes into view when we consider its double implication for the secularization thesis. On the one hand, it supports the hypothesis that religious institutions conform more and more to secularity and eventually lose their distinctiveness. This always occurs to some extent as growing and maturing religious groups accommodate themselves to the worldly demands of sustaining their enterprise. But the rise of medical magic goes beyond this in two important ways. First, it extends even to those sects and cults least accommodated to the world in other ways. Second, it represents the adoption by religion of secular models of reality as definitions of its mission, not just as useful tools to get along in the world. On those grounds, medical magic exemplifies the secularization of religion.

At the same time, though, medical magic involves a serious and rather systematic effort to resacralize the world, to "reenchant" the cosmos. It asserts the relevance of supernatural power at the very heart of one of secular society's most accomplished systems. Predicting a religious takeover of the healing arts would be unwarranted, but it is plausible to anticipate religion's gaining a respected and influential place in that secular world. Medical magic thus counters the conception of secularization as the decline of religion and its relegation to the limited private function of providing personal meaning.

By transcending the modern disjunction of sacred and secular, medical magic bids to define a new stage in the development both of religion and of modern society. To be sure, religious action incorporates more than just a sacred therapeutic, so a full assessment of these speculations awaits more comprehensive analysis. Nonetheless, religious groups articulate their earthly missions in the therapeutic models they adopt, which makes those ideas pivotal for locating religion in society. Medical magic may not change the character of the sacred entirely, but it has already shifted the position of religion among institutions. Sociologically at least, that move gives this new magic an advantage in setting religion's future course.

Unless it can gain dominance over previous models, however, the new therapy will not be able to capitalize on that advantage. And thus far, the rise of medical magic appears to have yielded only a greater pluralism of religious healing, not a new regime. The cure of souls is far from dead as a guide to ministry, and the belief in healing power seems to have flourished recently, even in established churches. If Weber's analysis is correct, though, we can expect healing power to rise and fall periodically like all charismatic phenomena, leaving the other two models to contend for historical dominance of ordinary life. In that contest, it would be unwise to bet against medical magic for its combination of sacred and secular gives religion unique adaptive fitness for advanced society. Its secularity makes it plausible to modern individuals as a response to their troubled existence, and its sacredness makes that response more powerful to them than mundane expertise alone. To that extent, medical magic may not only guide the development of religious culture but also establish a reference point for human existence in advanced societies.

REFERENCES

Abbott, Andrew. 1980. "Religion, psychiatry and problems of everyday life." *Sociological Analysis* 41, 2:164-171.

Bainbridge, William Sims. 1978. Satan's Power: A Deviant Psychotherapy Cult. Berkeley: University of California.

Bainbridge, William Sims and Rodney Stark. 1980. "Scientology: To be perfectly clear." *Sociological Analysis* 41, 2:128-136.

Crane, Diana. 1975. The Sanctity of Social Life: Physicians' Treatment of Critically Ill Patients. New Brunswick, N.J.: Transaction.

Fox, Renee C. 1979. Essays in Medical Sociology. New York: Wiley.

Goetting, Paul F. 1980. "The Christian congregation as a healing community." Pp. 77-90 in Henry L. Lettermann (ed.), Health and Healing. Chicago: Wheat Ridge Foundation.

Hadden, Jeffrey K. and Charles E. Swann. 1981. Prime Time Preachers: The Rising Power of Televangelism. Reading, Mass.: Addison-Wesley.

Hammond, Dorothy. 1970. "Magic: A problem in semantics." *American Anthropologist* 72, 6:1349-56.

Harrell, David Edwin, Jr. 1980. "Healing in Protestant America" Pp. 61-76 in Henry L. Lettermann (ed.), Health and Healing. Chicago: Wheat Ridge Foundation.

Harwood, Alan. 1977. Rx: Spiritist as Needed: A Study of a Puerto Rico Community Mental Health Resource. New York: Wiley.

Johnson, Benton. 1981. "A sociological perspective on the new religions." Pp. 51-66 in Thomas Robbins and Dick Anthony (ed.), In Gods We Trust: New Patterns of Religious Pluralism in America. New Brunswick: Transaction.

Larson, Donald H., with David E. Farely and Norman E. Minich. 1980. "Health and healing in the Lutheran Church: Tradition and practice." Pp. 43-60 in Henry L. Lettermann (ed.), Health and Healing. Chicago: Wheat Ridge Foundation.

Lettermann, Henry L. (ed.). 1980. Health and Healing: Ministry of the Church. Chicago: Wheat Ridge Foundation.

McGuire, Meredith B. 1981. Religion: The Social Context. Belmont, California: Wadsworth.

McNeill, John T. 1951. A History of the Cure of Souls. New York: Harper.

Moody, Edward. 1974. "Magical Therapy: An anthropological investigation of contemporary Satanism." Pp. 355-82 in I. Zaretsky and M. Leone (eds.), Religious Movements in Contemporary America. Princeton: Princeton U. Press.

Moore, Lorna G. and Peter W. Van Arsdale, JoAnne E. Glittenberg, and Robert A. Aldrich. 1980. The Biocultural Basis of Health. St. Louis: Mosby.

Peters, Edward. 1978. The Magician, the Witch and the Law. Philadelphia: University of Pennsylvania Press.

Robbins, Thomas and Dick Anthony. 1982. "Deprogramming, brainwashing and the medicalization of deviant religion." Social Problems 29:283-97.

Schneider, Louis, 1974. "The scope of 'the religious factor' and the sociology of religion: Notes on definition, idolatry and magic." Social Research 41, 2:340-61.

Siegler, Miriam and Humphrey Osmond. 1974. Models of Madness, Models of Medicine. New York: Harper.

Shriver, Donald W., Jr. 1980. Medicine and Religion: Strategies of Care. Pittsburgh: University of Pittsburgh.

Smith, Morton. 1978. Jesus the Magician. New York: Harper.

Telleen, Sharon. 1980. "The church as a support to families under stress." Pp. 91-108 in Henry L. Lettermann (ed.), Health and Healing. Chicago: Wheat Ridge Foundation.

Weber, Max. 1963. The Sociology of Religion. Tr. Ephraim Fischoff. Boston: Beacon.

Westberg, Granger E. 1980. "From hospital chaplaincy to wholistic health center." Pp. 109-116 in Henry L. Lettermann (ed.), Health and Healing. Chicago: Wheat Ridge Foundation.

10

TIME, IDENTITY, AND THE SPIRITUAL NEEDS OF THE ELDERLY

Michael Kearl

One manifestation of secularization that has achieved a "social problem" billing is the crisis of identity in old age. Assuming individuals require a sense of coherency and meaning to their lives, how is *biographical maintenance* (Berger and Luckmann, 1964:337) possible for those having experienced much social change during their lives and now facing death? This paper explicates this phenomenon by examining the social psychology of time. In so doing it seeks to realize a cross-fertilization of ideas between the sociologies of aging and religion, two ideal-type subjects of the sociology of knowledge. This approach to the humanistic concern for understanding biographical integrity and culmination (Moss, 1976), the "spiritual needs" of the elderly, is not to detract from parallel developmental conceptions of such psychologists as Erik Erikson (1950) and George A. Kelly (1955). Rather, it seeks to examine the social, particularly the religious, components of these psychological processes.

Both social and personal definitions of identity in old age have been studied by sociologists, psychologists, and gerontologists. All too frequently, however, the emphasis is on one or the other with less attention given to the dynamic interactions between identity and age. More specifically, while age norms and expectations (products of collective social action) are often cited as the basis for role continuity over time, and while personal conceptions of self are often cited as a product of the "generalized other" and responses to more immediate social relationships, this paper begins by exploring how the societal definitions of, and social reactions to, time *combine* to (1) enhance and reify the social order, and (2) stabilize and validate one's self conception. Self and society are indeed inseparable, but the delicate interaction of one with the other *over time* has been neglected in the literature. Identity is known to change with time as

I am indebted to Richard Machalek, David Oliver, Wilbert E. Moore, and John Donahue for helpful comments on earlier drafts of this paper. In addition, I would like to acknowledge the incisive comments of four anonymous readers who examined this article for the journal.

persons enter and exit from the social roles of life. But more importantly, as social definitions of those roles become altered historically the continuity of movement from one to the next can become problematic.[1] The focus here is to elaborate upon the dilemmas in maintaining biographical continuity in old age and thereby reveal the interdependencies of social histories with the changing personal identities across the life-cycle.

In developing time's role in providing coherency and comprehensibility (the sense of "order") to personal and social experiences, we will find ourselves engaged within the Weberian tradition of religious studies. From this perspective it will be shown how aged biographies have become problematical because of the pluralization of secular life course recipes which no longer tap the sacred temporality traditionally implicit within the religious rites of passage.

THE TEMPORAL STRUCTURE OF SOCIAL ORDER AND IDENTITY

The objective reality, as defined by society, is subjectively appropriated. In other words, socialization brings out symmetry between objective and subjective identity. The degree of this symmetry provides the criterion of the usefulness of socialization. The psychological reality of the successfully socialized individual thus verifies subjectively what his society defined as real (Berger, 1966:107).

To appreciate time's bearing upon the "problem" of old age we must first elaborate upon the social psychology and sociology of our temporality. Specifically, we will explain the role of time in shaping biographical coherence, comprehensibility, and culmination during the latter phase of life.

One sociological approach to the study of consciousness is to analyze the interpretative frameworks from which one derives meaning from one's experiences. This psychological process becomes sociological when the institutional and interactional sources of these interpretative models are identified. An emerging theoretical perspective portrays one's subjectivities to be dialectically related to a psychological model (assumed by the actor to be taken for granted among the others in the situation) which, in turn, is dialectically related to the social situation (Berger, 1966; Berger and Pullberg, 1965). In this way society can be said to order experiences.

Crucial to this entire process of fitting experiences within interpretative templates is the process of typification. We experience our social world and ourselves not in terms of the totality of stimuli but in terms of social recipes, or typifications (Schutz, 1973; Berger and Luckmann, 1966). Events are con-

[1] As Wilbert E. Moore (1963) observed, the increasing longevity of all classes in post-industrial societies has disrupted the centuries-old synchronization between the temporal order of social systems and the temporal order of biological man. Our contemporary social problem orientation to old age may exist in part because we now outlive the traditional lifespan "recipes" and no longer "know" how to grow old.

nected by conceptualization, not observation (McHugh, 1968). What is socially and personally meaningful is the conceptualization, not the observation. For me to share the experiences (and assume empathy on the part of my audience) of my adolescence, mid-career crisis, or old age, I must encapsulate that which is personally unique into common-currency symbolizations of temporal experiences. All social interaction is premised on this self-transcendence capability (Berger, 1969:55).

What eventually must be transcended are not mere discrete events, but the totality of situations experienced and anticipated by the individual. As Meerloo (1970:47) suggests, only children live in the present while the mature live simultaneously in the past, present, and future. The sense of identity, of self comprehensibility, is thus dependent upon this experience of temporal continuity.[2] "Psychoanalysis has taught us how the renewed experience of temporal connections between seemingly unrelated events alters the disturbing sense of unrelatedness and anxiety" (Meerloo, 1970:147). Cultural recipes exist by which discontinuities of experience are transcended, allowing the continuities to be brought out in sharp relief. These interpretative templates allow the individual to realize a socially standardized biographical model which gives continuity and meaning to oneself through time. In most societies, the form in which life experiences coalesce into personal epochs corresponds with some "stages-of-life" typification.

Cultural mythologies are replete with formulas by which the life cycle is typified. We can see the assumption of life stages in the riddle of the sphynx, in the "seasons of man," and in our demarcations of early or late adolescence and old age. However, because the biological process of aging is continuous, how do distinctive stages come to be recognized? Because man undergoes continual socio-psycho-biological change in his trajectory toward death, how are the implications of his changing existential self made socially meaningful, and how do these meanings change when the trajectory, itself, is modified? And finally, which institutions contribute to the distinctions and their ideological connotations?

In recent centuries chronological age has become the socially standardized basis for demarcating personal epochs. With the extensive differentiation and specialization of roles accompanying modernization, age has become the criterion by which role complexes have become linked together (Eisenstadt, 1956). It is the referent by which we can meaningfully distinguish a "five-

---

[2]Individuals and social systems are alike in that both seek continuity, and hence identity and meaning, through selective recollections. There are personal and collective rituals for forgetting and remembering (Mannheim, 1952). "We keep reinterpreting our biography very much as the Stalinists kept writing the Soviet Encyclopedia, calling forth some events into decisive importance as others were banished into ignominious oblivion" (Berger, 1963:57).

year-old'' from a "three-year-old," by which we can claim that an individual is either too young to be married or too old to be working full-time. Further, the way these age-linked stages of life are typified (which is another way of saying that one can calculate the age-appropriateness of a given activity) provides for the individual a standardized timetable by which one can gauge the "correctness" of one's life trajectory. From the actor's perspective, to be "on time" is to be socially synchronized in the sense above. To be "on time" implies an awareness of social structural time (Glaser and Strauss, 1971, 1965) and reveals the institutionalized bases of projects which make up one's *life plan*.

The life plan becomes a primary source of identity ... The life plan is the basic context in which knowledge of society is organized in the consciousness of the individual (Berger, Berger, Kellner, 1973:73).

The life plan becomes shaped by the timetables of those roles the individual most uses to compare himself with others. We are creatures of temporal comparison, contrasting our present selves with our former selves and with the biographies of significant others when they were at a comparable phase. Having been tracked with those of similar age through school, Little League, Girl Scouts, boot camp, and work, we come to ritually compare our biographical development with those of like age in our Christmas cards, alumni magazines, class reunions, and at professional meetings. The significance of such biographical comparisons has not only psychological but social consequences as well.

The significance of being "on time" not only provides the sense of biographical continuity but also reifies the social institutions shaping one's life plan. As we can see in Table 1, institutions in various ways demand biographical summaries. Assuming that identity is the product of reflection and that activities precede any insight into their biographical relevance, when the individual shapes his history in "institutionally relevant" ways he is simultaneously maintaining the institutional order of meanings upon which his symbolic identity depends. The clearest examples of this process are the pre-industrial rites-of-passage ceremonies described by anthropologist Arnold van Gennep (1969) wherein social identities are ritually transformed as to make biological changes socially and biographically meaningful. It is within these ceremonies we find the simultaneous reaffirmations of an individual's identity, the reality of one's new membership role within a social collectivity, and the reality of the group itself. The same processes are at work in the contemporary retirement ceremony when one's work history is described in the context of the company's history. Institutional episodes, or epochs, are objectivated within the biographical chapters of its members. For the individual, institutions may bring a symbolic order wherein one realizes a continuity of self through life and

TABLE 1

BIOGRAPHICAL TIMETABLES IMPLICIT IN THE LIFE PLAN

Institutions	Forms of Biographical Summaries	Rituals for Biographical Reviews of Self and Institution
FAMILY	Diaries, scrapbooks, memorabilia	Anniversaries, holidays, reminiscing of the old (life review), funerals
SCHOOL	Report cards, alumni magazines, applications for admittance	Annual award ceremonies, graduations, class reunions
WORK	Job vitae, portfolios of work histories, promotions and demotions	Annual evaluations and reviews, company indoctrination sessions when entering job, retirement ceremonies
ECONOMY	Credit histories, cancelled checks, possessions	Tax preparations
RELIGION	Rank in church hierarchy (deacon, elder, young adult, etc.)	Confessionals, Christmas and Easter, baptism, funerals

within the context of one's ancestors and successors (for example, the *Roots* phenomenon). The irony is that those with the greatest histories, having absorbed the greatest amount of social change and now facing the prospects of death, have generally been "disengaged" from those institutional support systems for biographical reaffirmations and interpretations. Old age has become the period of temporal individualism.

Related to the temporal problems of continuity in old age is the problem of biographical culmination. What final biographical chapter or epilogue is one to construct in order to punctuate the meaning of one's life story? Temporality involves not only rhythm, rate, and sequence (Sorokin, 1964), but beginnings and endings which together can shape the meanings of the in-between. Events of life can be likened to notes of music in that both have sequences of highs and lows. Change the tempo and duration of events and one changes the meaning of the whole. Further, any music composition or biography that fails to "correctly" culminate and end risks losing its overall comprehensibility. The case of old age may signal either a disengagement (which can be like the disruptive "exit trajectories" of high school seniors during the last week of class) or the beginning of life's deadline period for intense culminating activities (like the last week of legislative activities in Congress or the final two minutes of a football game). If we lay out our alloted three score and ten and match each decade with a day of the work week, the onset of old age can either be the Friday or Sunday of one's life. The meaning inferred temporally is part of what we know as culture, which is the "logico-meaningful" (Geertz, 1971) derivative of the institutional processes to which we are linked via our roles. Whether our deaths are to be premature, on-time, or post-mature is, then, a socially constructed idea.

From the perspective developed here, both social and personal orders depend upon coherent and properly culminated biographies. As we all must age and die, any cultural belief system that cannot provide security and self-esteem for those who face these natural sequences of life will have these limits revealed in the form of "social problem-types" when increasing numbers of individuals either outlive or violate in other ways the culture's life recipes. The "problem" of old age partially derives from the fact that in our secular, post-industrial, future-oriented society, the overarching sense of temporality the aging find in their biographies is *de*creasingly sacred and *in*creasingly profane.

THE SECULARIZATION OF TIME AND THE
EMERGENCE OF IDENTITY EXPERTS

The eschatological symbols are both the clearest and the most powerful expression of the Christian understanding of human temporality (Tracy, 1975:122).

Since aging involves the experience of time, any changes in time's meaning will be reflected in the meaning of old age. The argument is that the "aging problem" partially derives from the secularization and individualization of biographical timetables. This had led to the situation, as evidenced in Table 2, where both the young and the old perceive the first half of life to contain the best years.

If a basic function of society is the production of identities and the maintenance of self-esteem, this distribution of the "good years," across the life-cycle wherein everything is "downhill" from the forties on, must be explained and legitimated within the "context of the most general frame of reference conceivable" (Berger and Luckmann, 1966:99), if cultural life plans are to be nonproblematical and unquestioningly accepted. This is a type of problem addressed by the sociology of religion, a tradition we shall now apply.[3]

[3] In the Weberian tradition of religious studies, the problem of individual existence is perceived to be the religious problem *par excellence*. If we distinguish religious knowledge from religious institutional frameworks, "religion" can be understood as the "symbolic glue" (Bellah, 1970) which makes sense out of and gives meaning and order to the net sum of human activity. It

TABLE 2

THE BEST AND THE WORST YEARS OF LIFE AS SEEN
BY SAMPLINGS OF THE AMERICAN ADULT PUBLIC, 1974*

Years	The Best Years of Life			The Worst Years of Life		
	Total Public	18-64	65+	Total Public	18-64	65+
Teens	15%	16%	7%	18%	20%	10%
20s	31%	33%	17%	6%	5%	7%
30s	23%	24%	22%	3%	3%	5%
40s	14%	13%	17%	3%	3%	3%
50s	4%	3%	8%	5%	6%	4%
60s	2%	1%	6%	13%	12%	14%
70s	*	*	2%	21%	21%	21%
Other	1%	1%	2%	6%	6%	7%
Wouldn't choose	8%	7%	15%	18%	17%	22%
Not sure	2%	2%	4%	7%	7%	7%

Source: Harris, 1975:2,12.

When the church had monopoly over the moral order, it ritualistically integrated biographical episodes with social episodes through its rites-of-passage. Religious knowledge provided coherency, continuity, and overarching comprehensibility to the meanings of social-historical and personal-biographical events. It provided ideological templates by which one's past experiences could be sedimented so as to reveal the sacred story implicit in one's biography (Novak, 1971:44-52). How, in part, discrete life events could be integrated involves the religious structuring of temporal orientations. This occurs on two levels.

On the cultural level, the role of time in religious knowledge and rituals is to assist in the demarcation of the sacred and the profane (Durkheim, 1965). What is sacred is the order that links our activities with an overarching meaning. To accurately repeat the rituals of one's ancestors, for example, is to participate in scared time. Sacred time is the collapse of the past and future into an eternal now: the heroics of our ancestors and our descendants will forever be part of the present. Profane time is passing time, time as decay or entropy, time without immortality. Where the life-cycle is infused with religious immanence, old age has sacred meaning.

integrates the social system functions (the moral order without) with the personality system functions (the moral order within) (Berger, 1969). From this perspective, the "soul" can be understood to be identity, and the traditional activity of "religion" to be soul, or biographical, maintenance.

On the personal-psychological level, what is sacred is the order religious knowledge gives to one's biography. Berger writes "the experience of conversion to a meaning system that is capable of ordering the scattered data of one's biography is liberating and profoundly satisfying" (1963:63). When the church had monopoly over most institutions it had monopoly over the life plans of individuals. Its rites-of-passage synchronized within a single ritual the biological, the social, and the cultural time frameworks.[4] And old age could be legitimated as the reward for living a morally correct life.

With the increasing differentiation and specialization of the occupational structure, life plans became pluralized (Neugarten and Hagestad, 1976:37). Concomitantly, the individualization of biographical timetables has been accompanied by their secularization. The biographical reviews demanded of the individual by the various institutions summarized in Table 1, the rational accountings and justifications of one's past, are now typically devoid of overarching, sacred meaning. The social rituals and props for assisting the individual in realizing biographical continuity and culmination have faded. In part this is because the referent by which we gauge the "correctness" of our life course, the organizing principle of our biographies, now derives from work and not from some imagined cosmic rhythm. The meaning of our lives is generally no longer seen as a means toward enhancing social solidarities nor as a means toward some immortal reward for living the "full life." Old age is no longer sacred because of its past nor its proximity to the hereafter, but profane as it implies completion of the full life opportunities.

The "problem" of old age derives, in part, because its life-stage meaning does not follow the progressive logic of the other, productivity-oriented stages of life. Implicit within these earlier stages is a temporally structured mobility plan (Becker and Strauss, 1968; Berger and Pullberg, 1965): each year of school is predicated upon the previous years' training and anticipates the following; high school is a stepping stone to college; the college diploma is the license for advanced training; education is assumed to lead to work, wherein one "moves up" through a hierarchy of achievement levels, and so on.

The mobility ethos, by contrast with values that are bound to the family or a subculture, is one of the few norms continuously reaffirmed in the life of the individual and thus taking on for him the character of massive reality (Berger and Luckmann, 1964:340).

Old age is understood as that time when mobility not only runs out, but turns "downward."

---

[4] We can still see the social psychology of religion's management of biographical temporality in the confessional. Here the contamination of one's future self by one's past selves is ritually prevented. The individual is free to experience a "fresh start," to begin a new chapter of his autobiography and understand the deviant past as but a footnote of one's story.

The secular theodicy that has emerged to justify this stratification of mobility is retirement. Retirement is in this country an economic and *moralistic* vindication for growing old, a time for individualism that one supposedly "earns" for having fulfilled one's social obligations. But individualism does not lessen the need for meaning and coherency of one's biography, the desire for self-esteem, nor the fear of death. The old, the self-proclaimed "pioneers" of a new stage of life, must now shop around for life recipes in the secular marketplace of identity experts (Berger, 1965:37; Berger and Luckmann, 1964:337). With the increasing specialization within the service sector of the division of labor, the church has become unable to retain its historical monopoly over "soul management" when challenged by the scientifically legitimated experts such as psychologists, job counselors, and gerontologists.

The changing nature of work has not only contributed to the causes of old age identity problems (as through limited mobility, mandatory retirements, and the obsolescence of work skills), but has shaped the *form* by which they are understood. A consequence of the secularization of biographical experts has been the application of therapeutic metaphors to understand and "treat" deviance: the religious distinction of the sacred and profane has metamorphized into a healthy-unhealthy dichotomy (Freidson, 1970). One is no longer a drunkard but is an alcoholic, a student is no longer "dumb" but suffers instead from a "learning disability," and the disoriented senior is not so much a victim of social structure but rather of "senility." [5]

Not too surprisingly, we are witnessing the creation of novel typifications for the subjective experiences and anticipations of growing old. One type of biographical experience, the sensation of periodic "crises" across the life-cycle, has increasingly become therapeutized, institutionalized as a "normal" event requiring "typical treatment." The so-called "mid-career crisis," the first symptom of old age, is a case in point. Job counselors, marriage counselors, syndicated advice columnists, psychiatrists, and even physicians (some of whom are now talking of mid-life hormonal changes in males) have reaffirmed the "reality" of the phenomenon though with distinctive interpretations and prescriptions.

The old represent the moral problems posed by poor health, the nucleated family, poverty, leisure, and boredom, and they have accordingly become recognized as the ideal-type service recipients. They (and those worrying about being one of them) are a resource to be competed for by differing therapeutic

[5] A further implication of this service sector absorption of biographical recipes is that any "social improvement" occurs not through institutional reconstruction, but through the modification of individuals. The social structure has come to shape recognized identities through institutionalized psychologisms which have become not only "sciences" but techniques of rational control with "health, education, personal mobility, or psychological healing . . . (becoming) defined as the result of services or 'treatments' " (Illich, 1971:2).

strategies. Since many individuals do not "know" how to grow old and since those who are now old are not generally recognized as role models,[6] the primacy of the secondary institutions, the new moral entrepreneurs, in providing recipes for aging cannot be overstated. "The need for therapy increases in proportion to the structurally-given potentiality for unsuccessful socialization" (Berger and Luckmann, 1966:168). Accordingly, the way the old are popularly typified, the way their place in society is understood, is not in terms of their individualism nor their wisdom through maturity, but in terms of their service needs.

CONCLUSION

Time has a constituent role in shaping our apprehensions of "reality." There is a temporal order implicit in our roles, interactions, histories, and cognitions. Seeing so much of the gerontological enterprise being engaged in studying the effects and experiences of time, social psychologists of aging need to develop more fully the bearing of social and cultural temporal systems on identity. They must note the parallels between the dynamics of "leave-taking" from a social situation and retirement, and they must develop models of not only socialization but desocialization. Further, unless they are willing to argue that life is but a series of atomistic "nows," they must identify those institutional support systems contributing to the maintenance of biographical continuity and comprehensibility.[7] In so doing it will be realized the extent to which institutional orders are reified, or made real, within the biographical reflections of individuals.

With the fading of religious immanence of our everyday life and with the increase of individualism (of which retirement is an ideal-type form), biographical maintenance has become a personal project. For the individual, the urges of introspection and of temporal comparisons of self through time seem to be correlated with education, increases of which diminish one's self-taken-for-grantedness and intensify one's phenomenological concerns with self

[6] The Louis Harris survey of 4254 Americans shows only 23 percent of the total public believing that talking with an older person is very helpful in preparing for one's own later years (Harris, 1975).

[7] With this orientation we can theoretically integrate such diverse findings as the correlation between retirement morale and the orderliness of one's work history (Simpson, Back, and McKinney, 1966) and the referral patterns of clergy when handling life cycle transitions (Cumming and Harrington, 1963). In the search for indices of spiritual well-being (Moberg, 1979), researchers may well be advised to study the bearing of religious knowledge in providing biographical continuity, comprehensibility, and coherence. One methodological tactic may be to measure rank-orderings of identity experts in terms of their perceived ability to assist in various "crises" of the life cycle. Another is to further develop the methodology of oral histories, content analyzing those institutional themes which individuals not only see as being the most central events of their lives, but which organize long lifetimes of discrepant experiences.

change (Lopata, 1973). In our search for overarching continuity to our multiplicity of life timetables, we increasingly turn to secular identity experts who tell us how to monitor our psychological "health," how to "self-actualize" ourselves, and how to grow old. With different cohorts growing old in distinctive ways within a constantly changing society, it seems these "soul therapists" will be in continual demand for designing new recipes by which to grow old. However, unless these secular identity experts can capture the experience of sacred temporality formerly implicit within our biographies, their efforts may be doomed to failure.

REFERENCES

Becker, H. S., and A. Strauss. 1968. "Careers, personality, and adult socialization." Pp. 311-320 in B. Neugarten (ed.), *Middle Age and Aging: A Reader in Social Psychology*. Chicago: University of Chicago.

Bellah, R. N. 1970. Beyond Belief. New York: Harper and Row.

Berger, P. 1963. Invitation to Sociology. Garden City: Doubleday.

1965. "Towards a sociological understanding of psychoanalysis." *Social Research*. 32:26-41.

1966. "Identity as a problem in the sociology of knowledge." *Archives Europeanes De Sociologie*. 7:105-115.

1969. The Sacred Canopy. Garden City: Doubleday.

Berger, P., and T. Luckmann. 1964. "Social mobility and personal identity." *European Journal of Sociology*. 5:331-344.

1966. The Social Construction of Reality. Garden City: Doubleday.

Berger, P., and S. Pullberg. 1965. "Reification and the sociological critique of consciousness." *History and Theory* 4:196-211.

Berger, P., B. Berger, and H. Kellner. 1973. The Homeless Mind: Modernization and Consciousness. New York: Random House.

Cumming, E., and C. Harrington. 1963. "Clergyman as counselor." *American Journal of Sociology* 69:234-243.

Durkheim, E. 1965. The Elementary Forms of the Religious Life. New York: Free Press.

Eisenstadt, S. N. 1965. From Generation to Generation. New York: Free Press.

Erikson, E. 1950. Childhood and Society. New York: Norton.

Freidson, E. 1970. Profession of Medicine: A Study in the Sociology of Applied Knowledge. New York: Dodd, Mead.

Geertz, C. 1973. The Interpretation of Cultures. New York: Basic.

Glaser, B., and A. Strauss, 1971. Status Passage. Chicago: Aldine Atherton.

1965. "Temporal aspects of dying as a non-scheduled status passage." *American Journal of Sociology* 71:48-59.

Harris, Louis, and Associates. 1975. The Myth and Reality of Aging in America. National Council of the Aging.

Illich, I. 1971. Deschooling Society. New York: Harper and Row.

Kelly, G. A. 1955. The Psychology of Personal Constructs. New York: Norton.

Lopata, H. 1973. "Self-identity in marriage and widowhood." *The Sociological Quarterly* 14:407-408.

McHugh, P. 1968. Defining the Situation: The Organization of Meaning in Social Interaction. New York: Macmillan.

Mannheim, K. 1952. "The problem of generations." In P. Kecskemeti (ed. and tr.) *Essays on the Sociology of Knowledge.* London: Routledge and Kegan Paul.

Meerloo, J. A. M. 1970. Along the Fourth Dimension. New York: John Day.

Moberg, D. 1979. Spiritual Well-Being: Sociological Perspectives. Washington, D.C.: University Press.

Moore, W. E. 1963. Man, Time, and Society. New York: Wiley.

Moss, W. G. 1976. Humanistic Perspectives on Aging. Institute of Gerontology. The University of Michigan-Wayne State.

Neugarten, B., and G. Hagestad. 1976. "Age and the life course." Pp. 35-55 in Binstock and E. Shanas (eds.), *Handbook of Aging and the Social Sciences.* New York: Nostrand.

Novak, M. 1971. "Religion as autobiography." In M. Novak, *Ascent of the Mountain, Flight of the Dove.* New York: Harper and Row.

Schutz, A. 1973. Collected Papers I. Hague: I. Martinus Nijhoff.

Simpson, I. H., McKinney, J., and Back, K. 1966. "Attitudes of work, involvement in society, and self-evaluation in retirement." Pp. 55-74 in Simpson, McKinney, et al. (eds.), *Social Aspects of Aging.* Durham, N.C.: Duke.

Sorokin, P. A. 1964. Sociocultural Casuality, Space, Time: A Study of Referential Principles of Sociology and Social Science. New York: Russell and Russell.

Tracy, D. 1975. "Eschatological perspectives on aging." In S. Hiltner (ed.), *Toward a Theology of Aging.* New York: Human Science Press.

van Gennep, A. 1969. The Rites of Passage. Chicago: University of Chicago.